JUMP Math 3.2

Book 3 Part 2 of 2

Contents

jump math™

MULTIPLYING POTENTIAL.

JUMP Math
One Yonge Street, Suite 1014
Toronto, Ontario M5E 1E5
Canada
www.jumpmath.org

Writers: Francisco Kibedi, Dr. Anna Klebanov, Saverio Mercurio, Dr. John Mighton
Consultants: Dr. Anna Klebanov, Dr. Sohrab Rahbar, Dr. Sindi Sabourin
Editors: Megan Burns, Liane Tsui, Natalie Francis, Jackie Dulson, Janice Dyer, Laura Edlund, Dawn Hunter, Neomi Majmudar, Una Malcolm, Rachelle Redford
Layout and Illustrations: Linh Lam, Fely Guinasao-Fernandes, Sawyer Paul, Audrey Chia
Cover Design: Blakeley Words+Pictures
Cover Photograph: © iStockphoto.com/Michael Kemter

ISBN 978-1-927457-43-6

Second printing July 2017

Printed and bound in Canada

Welcome to JUMP Math

Entering the world of JUMP Math means believing that every child has the capacity to be fully numerate and to love math. Founder and mathematician John Mighton has used this premise to develop his innovative teaching method. The resulting resources isolate and describe concepts so clearly and incrementally that everyone can understand them.

JUMP Math is comprised of teacher's guides (which are the heart of our program), interactive whiteboard lessons, student assessment & practice books, evaluation materials, outreach programs, and teacher training. The Common Core Editions of our resources have been carefully designed to cover the Common Core State Standards. All of this is presented on the JUMP Math website: **www.jumpmath.org**.

Teacher's guides are available on the website for free use. Read the introduction to the teacher's guides before you begin using these resources. This will ensure that you understand both the philosophy and the methodology of JUMP Math. The assessment & practice books are designed for use by students, with adult guidance. Each student will have unique needs and it is important to provide the student with the appropriate support and encouragement as he or she works through the material.

Allow students to discover the concepts by themselves as much as possible. Mathematical discoveries can be made in small, incremental steps. The discovery of a new step is like untangling the parts of a puzzle. It is exciting and rewarding.

Students will need to answer the questions marked with a 📓 in a notebook. Grid paper notebooks should always be on hand for answering extra questions or when additional room for calculation is needed.

Contents

PART 1

Unit 4: Operations and Algebraic Thinking: Skip Counting and Multiplication

Unit 5: Operations and Algebraic Thinking: Multiplication

Unit 6: Measurement and Data: Perimeter and Area

Unit 7: Operations and Algebraic Thinking: Operations with Money

Unit 8: Operations and Algebraic Thinking: Division

PART 2
Unit 1: Geometry: Shapes

Unit 2: Number and Operations—Fractions: Fractions

Unit 3: Operations and Algebraic Thinking: Unknown Numbers

Unit 4: Number and Operations in Base Ten: Rounding and Estimating

Unit 5: Measurement and Data: Time

Unit 6: Measurement and Data: Length in US Customary Units

Unit 7: Measurement and Data: Area in US Customary Units

Unit 8: Measurement and Data: Volume and Mass

Unit 9: Measurement and Data: Graphs

G3-1 Sides and Vertices of Shapes

Triangles and squares are flat shapes. Flat shapes have **sides** and **vertices**.
A **vertex** is where two sides meet.

1. Draw ✓ on each side. Write the number of sides.

a)

___3___ sides

b)

___4___ sides

c)

___4___ sides

d)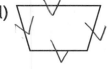

___4___ sides

e)

_12_ sides

f)

___7___ sides

2. Circle each vertex. Write the number of vertices.

a)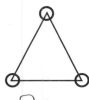

___3___ vertices

b)

___4___ vertices

c)

___4___ vertices

d)

___4___ vertices

e)

_12_ vertices

f)

___7___ vertices

3. Write the number of sides and vertices.

a)

___5___ sides
___5___ vertices

b)

___4___ sides
___4___ vertices

c)

___6___ sides
___6___ vertices

A **polygon** is a closed shape with straight sides only.

Polygons   Not polygons

 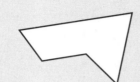 |

4. Is the shape a polygon? Hint: Look at the examples above.

a)

_____no_____

b)

_____yes_____

c)

___ћ0___

d)

___✓___

e)

___✓___

f)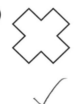

___✓___

g)

___✗___

h)

___✗___

5. Use a ruler. Draw a polygon with the given number of sides or vertices.

a) 3 sides   b) 5 sides   c) 4 vertices

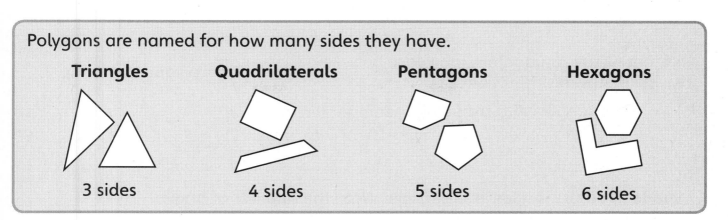

Polygons are named for how many sides they have.

| Triangles | Quadrilaterals | Pentagons | Hexagons |
| 3 sides | 4 sides | 5 sides | 6 sides |

6. Complete the table using the shapes on the right.

Shape	Examples
Triangle	A, F
Quadrilateral	B d
Pentagon	g I E
Hexagon	C
Not a polygon	H

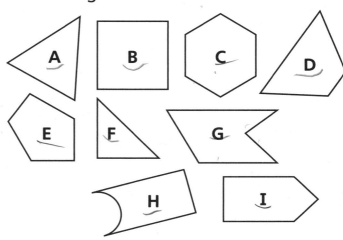

7. a) Draw a shape with 4 sides that is not a polygon.

b) Is your shape a quadrilateral?

   yes

c) Explain your answer to part b).

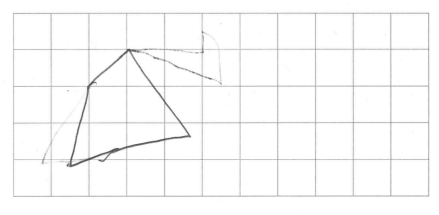

8. How many sides does a stop sign have? ___6___

Is this shape a polygon? ___✓___

BONUS ▶ Can you draw a polygon where the number of

sides does not equal the number of vertices? ___✗___

In a flat shape, an angle is the space between two straight sides that meet at a vertex.

Clara shows angles in a shape by shading them in.

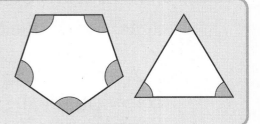

1. Shade in all the angles in the shape. Write the number of angles inside the shape.

a)

5

b)
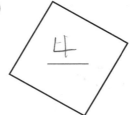
4

c)

7

d)

4

e)

3

f)
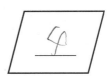
4

g)

5

h)
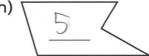
5

i)
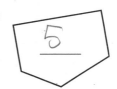
5

2. Count the angles inside the shape. Then count the vertices.

a)
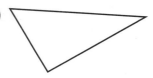

_____ angles

_____ vertices

b)
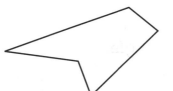

_____ angles

_____ vertices

c)
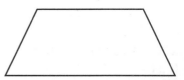

_____ angles

_____ vertices

3. Clara says that polygons have the same number of angles as vertices.

Is she correct? _____

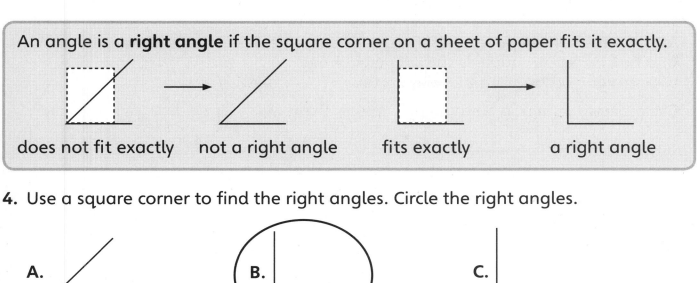

An angle is a **right angle** if the square corner on a sheet of paper fits it exactly.

does not fit exactly   not a right angle   fits exactly   a right angle

4. Use a square corner to find the right angles. Circle the right angles.

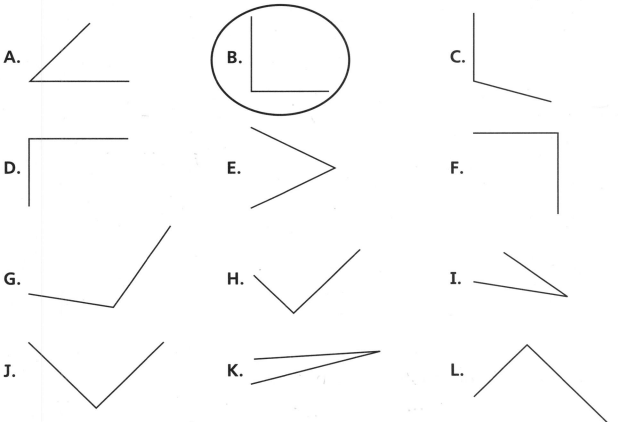

A.

B.

C.

D.

E.

F.

G.

H.

I.

J.

K.

L.

5. Use a ruler to draw the given angle.

a) a right angle

b) not a right angle

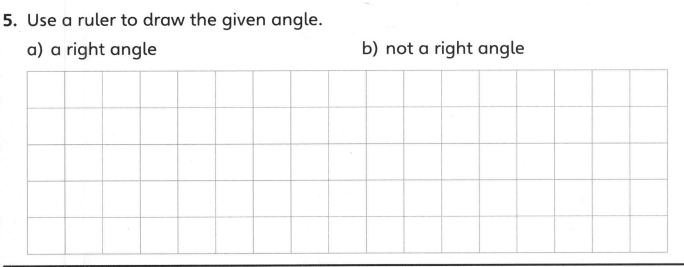

To show that an angle is a right angle, you can draw a small square in it.

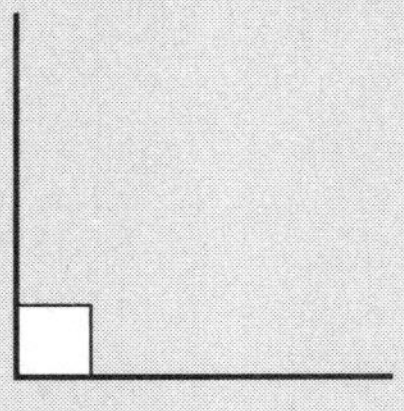

Right angle 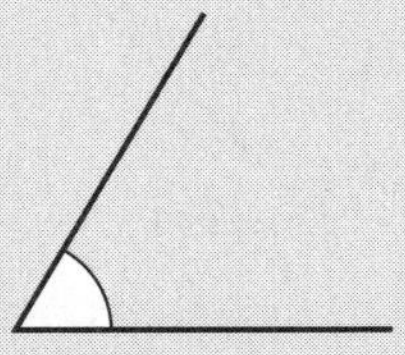   Not a right angle

6. Draw a small square in each right angle. Write the number of right angles inside the shape.

a)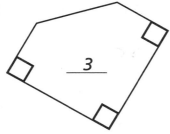
_3_

b)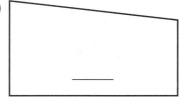
_____

c)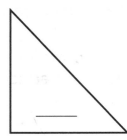
_____

d)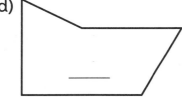
_____

e)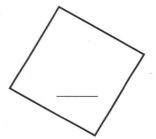
_____

f)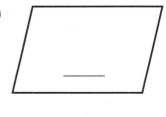
_____

7. Draw a small square in each right angle in the picture. One of the squares has been drawn for you.

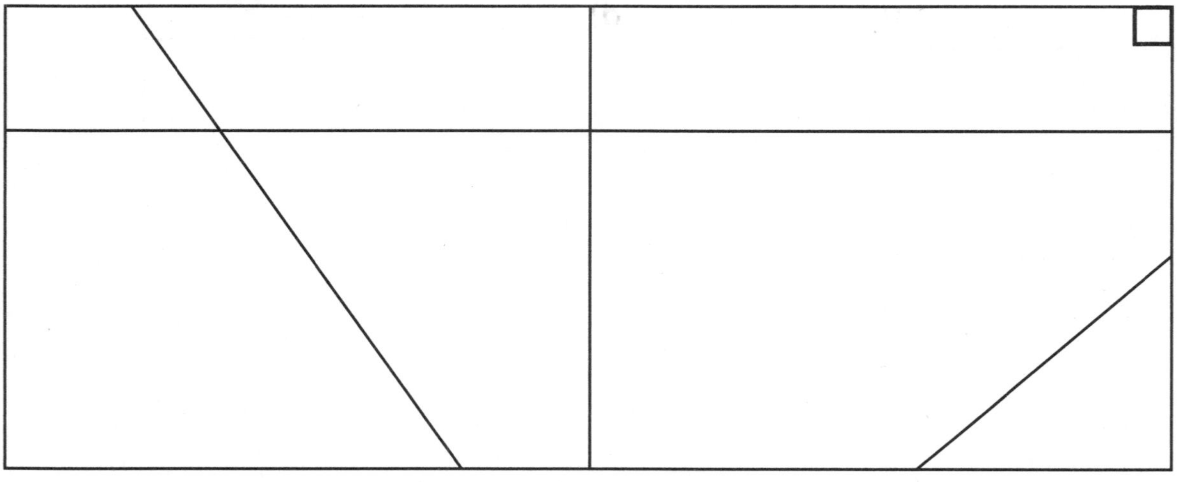

G3-3 Shapes with Equal Sides

You can measure the sides of a shape to find out if it has sides of equal length.

4 cm

2 cm | **A** | 2 cm

4 cm

Not all sides are equal in length

3 cm

3 cm | **B** | 3 cm

3 cm

All sides are equal in length

I. Use a ruler to measure the sides in centimeters. Are the sides equal in length or not equal?

a)

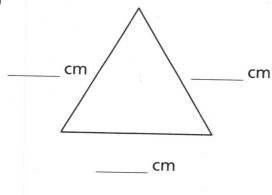

_____ cm

_____ cm

_____ cm

_____ *equal* _____

b)

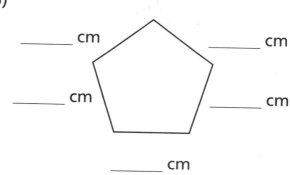

_____ cm   _____ cm

_____ cm   _____ cm

_____ cm

_____

c)

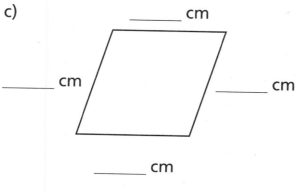

_____ cm

_____ cm

_____ cm

_____ cm

_____

d)

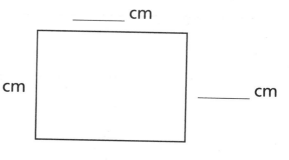

_____ cm

_____ cm   _____ cm

_____ cm

_____

Ben draws hash marks on the sides of shapes to show which sides are equal. Sides that have the same number of hash marks are equal.

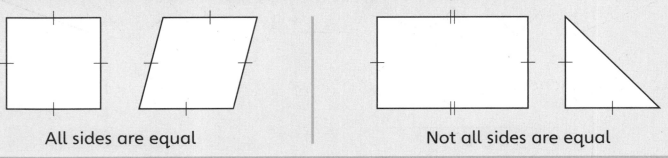

All sides are equal   Not all sides are equal

2. Draw hash marks to show which sides are equal.

a)

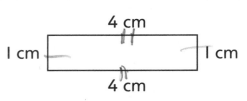

b)

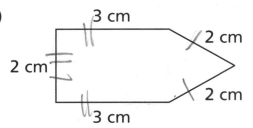

3. a) Measure the sides of each shape in centimeters. Draw hash marks to show which sides are equal.

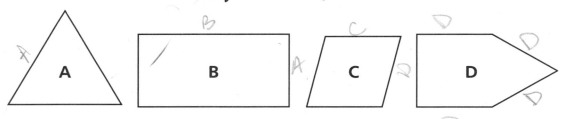

b) Write the letter for each shape in part a) where it belongs in the table.

All sides are equal	A C D
Not all sides are equal	B

4. Draw a shape with the given number of sides. Each shape must have not all equal sides.

a) 3 sides   b) 4 sides

BONUS ▶ Draw a shape that has four equal sides and is not a square.

5.

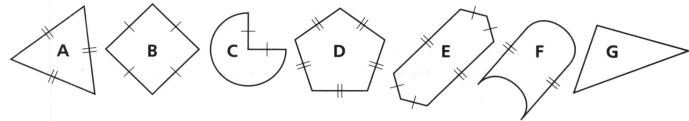

a) Which shapes are polygons? Hint: a polygon is a shape with

straight sides. _A B D E G_

b) Which shapes have all sides equal? _AB D_

Yu describes shapes by their name, and by **all sides equal** or **not all sides equal**.

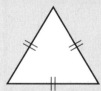

Triangle with all sides equal 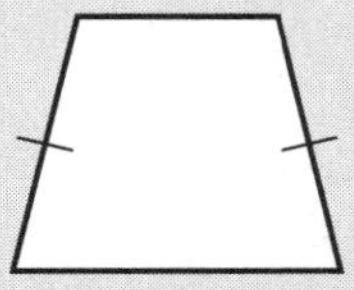   Quadrilateral with not all sides equal

6. Does the polygon have all sides equal or not all sides equal?
Write the name of the polygon.

a)

All sides equal

Quadrilateral

b)

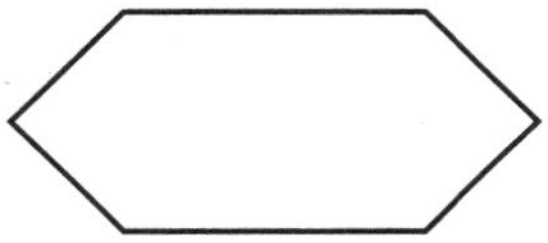

Not

Hexdgon

c)

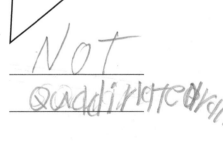

Not

Quadirlratearus

d)

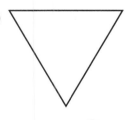

yuP

triAnole

e)

NoT

Taiangle

f)

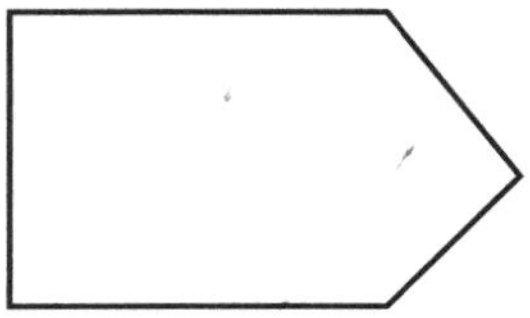

NoT

Polygon

G3-4 Quadrilaterals

> **REMINDER** ▶ A polygon with 4 sides is called a **quadrilateral**.

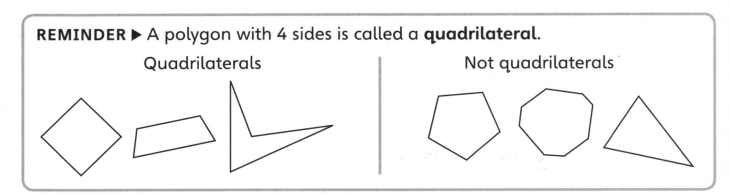

Quadrilaterals | Not quadrilaterals

1. Count the number of sides for each shape. Then write the letter for each shape where it belongs in the table.

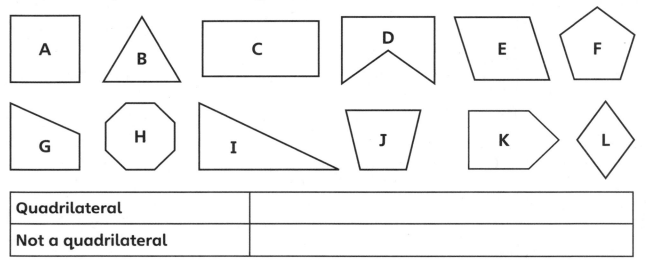

Quadrilateral	
Not a quadrilateral	

> **REMINDER** ▶ Sides in a shape marked with the same number of hash marks are equal. Angles marked with a small square are right angles.

2.

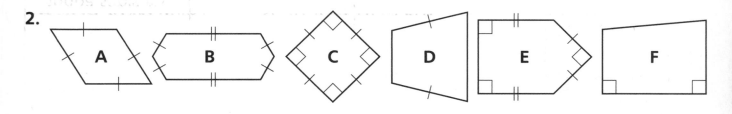

a) Which shapes are quadrilaterals? _____

b) Which shapes have all sides equal? _____

c) Which shapes have right angles? _____

A **rectangle** has:
- 4 sides
- 4 right angles

Rectangles are quadrilaterals with 4 right angles.

3. Write ✓ for what is true. Is the shape a rectangle?

a)

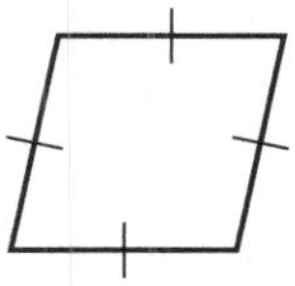

[✓] Quadrilateral

[ ] 4 right angles

Rectangle? ___no___

b)

[ ] Quadrilateral

[ ] 4 right angles

Rectangle? _____

c)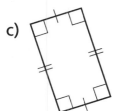

[ ] Quadrilateral

[ ] 4 right angles

Rectangle? _____

d)

[ ] Quadrilateral

[ ] 4 right angles

Rectangle? _____

4. a) Which shape in Question 3 is a square? _____

b) Is the square a rectangle? _____

5. Complete the table.

	Quadrilateral? 4 sides	Rectangle? 4 sides 4 right angles	Square? 4 sides 4 right angles All sides equal
a) 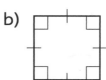	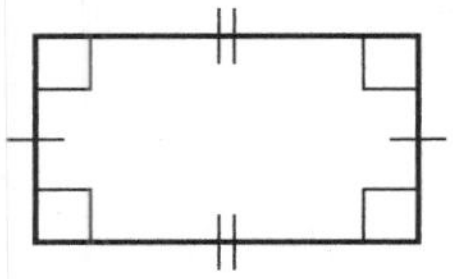 yes	yes	no
b) 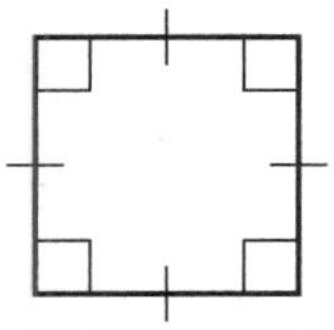			
c) 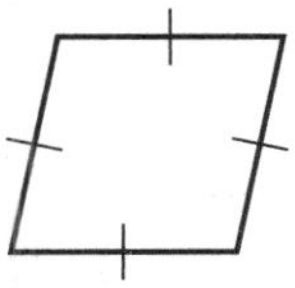 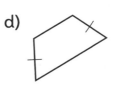			

6. Write ✓ if the shape is a rectangle. Write ✗ if the shape is not a rectangle.

a)

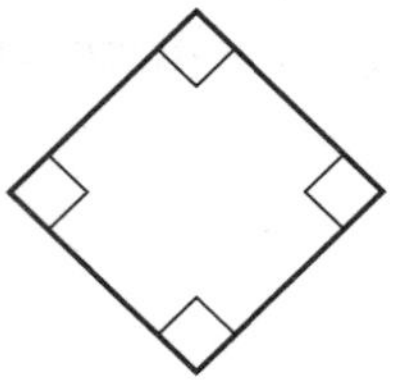

b)

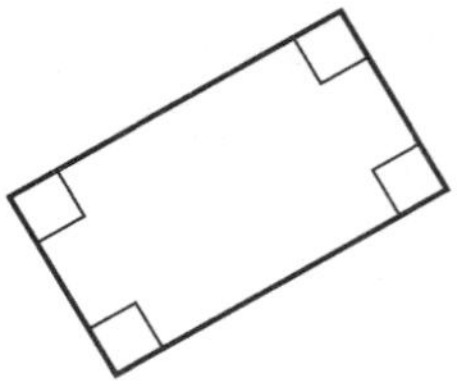

c)

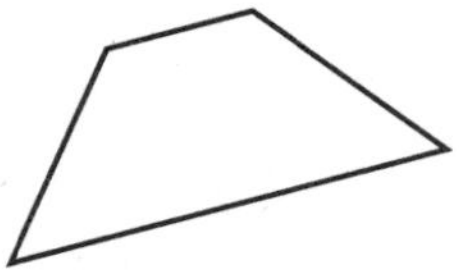

d)

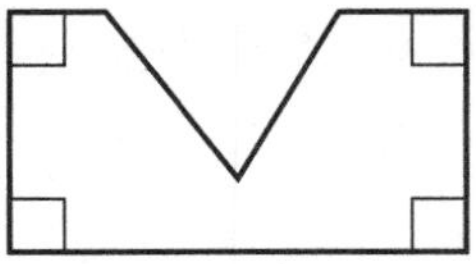

☐ Rectangle   ☐ Rectangle   ☐ Rectangle   ☐ Rectangle

7. Use a ruler to draw a rectangle that is not a square.

8. Use a ruler to draw a quadrilateral that is not a rectangle.

9. Are all squares rectangles? Explain how you know.

_____

_____

_____

G3-5 More Quadrilaterals

A **rhombus** has:
- 4 sides
- all sides equal

Another way to say this is:
Rhombuses are quadrilaterals with all sides equal.

1. Write ✓ for what is true. Is the shape a rhombus?

a)
   - ☑ Quadrilateral
   - ☑ All sides equal

   Rhombus? ___yes___

b)
   - ☐ Quadrilateral
   - ☐ All sides equal

   Rhombus? _____

c)
   - ☐ Quadrilateral
   - ☐ All sides equal

   Rhombus? _____

d)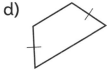
   - ☐ Quadrilateral
   - ☐ All sides equal

   Rhombus? _____

2. a) Which shape in Question 1 is a square? _____

   b) Is the square a rhombus? _____

3. Complete the table.

	Quadrilateral? 4 sides	Rhombus? 4 sides All sides equal	Square? 4 sides 4 right angles All sides equal
a)	yes	no	no
b)			
c)			

4. Are all squares rhombuses? Explain how you know.

5. Complete the table.

	Rectangle? 4 sides 4 right angles	Rhombus? 4 sides All sides equal	Square? 4 sides 4 right angles All sides equal
a) 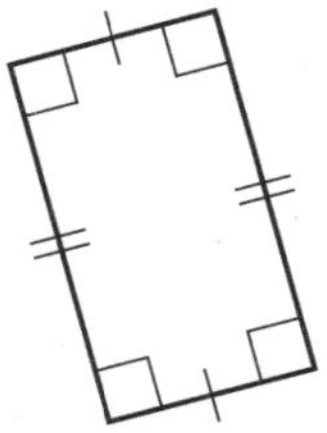			
b) 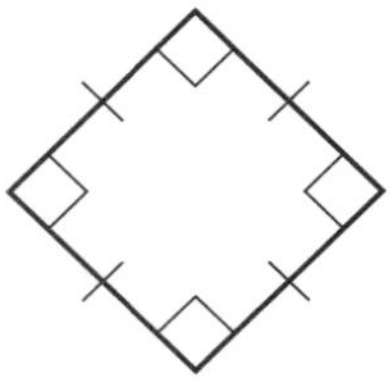			
c) 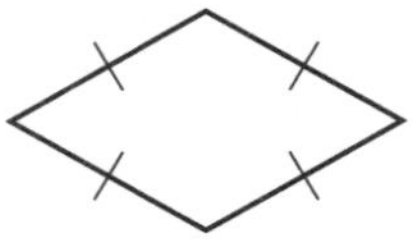			
d) 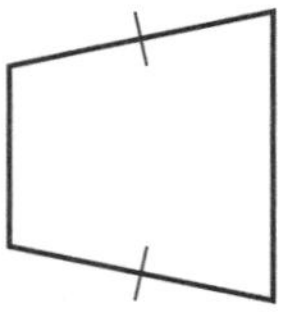			
e) 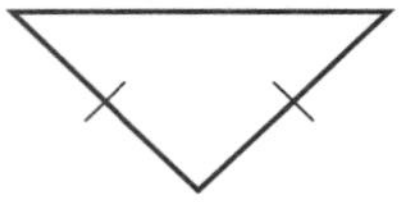			

BONUS ▶ Write all the names that describe the shape. Use "quadrilateral," "rectangle," "rhombus," and "square."

a)

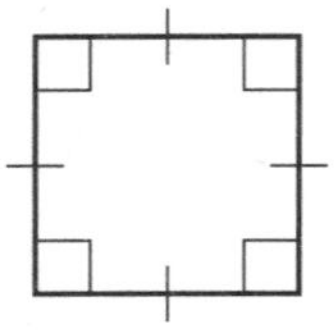

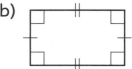

b)

c)

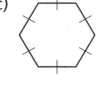

_____

_____

_____

_____

6. Use a ruler to draw a quadrilateral with the given angles or sides.

a) 1 right angle

b) no right angles

c) no sides equal

d) 2 sides equal

7. Use a ruler to draw a rectangle with the given sides.

a) 2 short sides and 2 long sides

b) all sides equal

BONUS ▶ Bo drew two quadrilaterals.

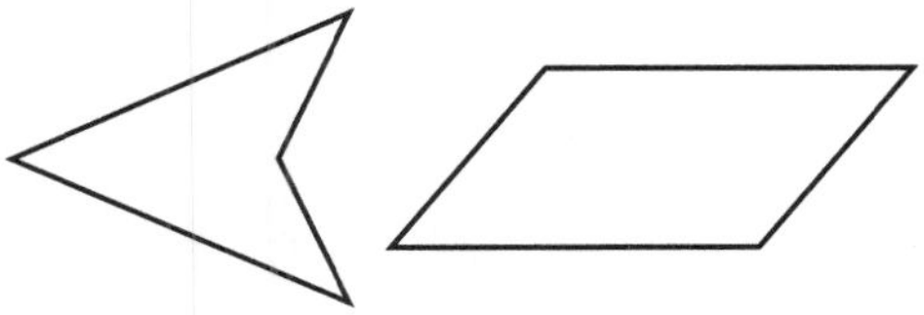

They have 2 equal long sides, 2 equal short sides, and are not rectangles.

Draw another shape like this in the grid.

G3-6 Parallel Sides

Parallel sides are like straight railroad tracks: they go in the same direction and are the same distance apart everywhere.

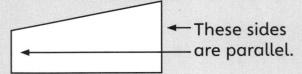 ←These sides are parallel.

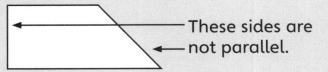 These sides are not parallel.

1. Are the thicker sides parallel?

a)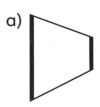

_____yes_____

b)

_____

c)

_____

d)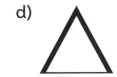

_____

e)

_____

f)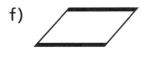

_____

g)

_____

h)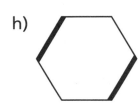

_____

2. The picture shows 2 parallel sides. Join the dots to make a quadrilateral.

a)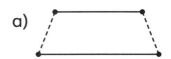

b)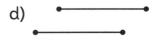

c)

d)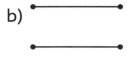

e)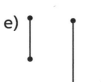

f)

g)

h)

i)

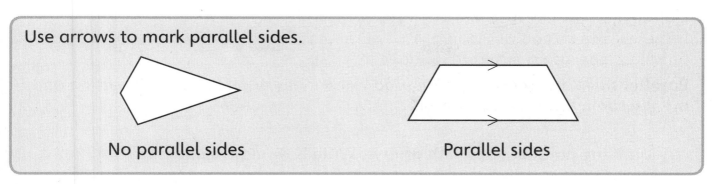

Use arrows to mark parallel sides.

No parallel sides   Parallel sides

3. Mark the parallel sides with arrows.

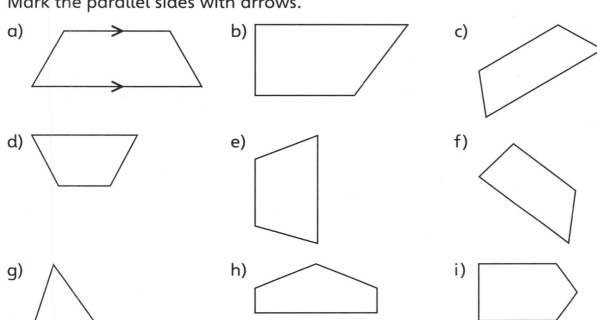

a)   b)   c)

d)   e)   f)

g)   h)   i)

4. Draw a quadrilateral with the given sides.

a) one pair of parallel sides   b) no parallel sides

> If there is more than one pair of parallel sides, use a different number of arrows for each pair.

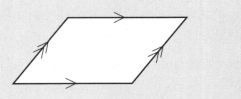

5. a) Mark the parallel sides with arrows. Write how many pairs of sides are parallel.

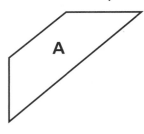
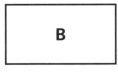
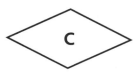
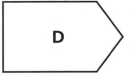

_____   _____   _____   _____

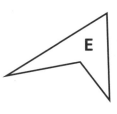

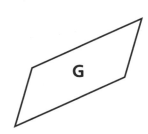
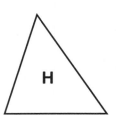

_____   _____   _____   _____

b) Write the letter for each shape in part a) where it belongs in the table.

No pairs of parallel sides	
One pair of parallel sides	
Two pairs of parallel sides	

> Parallel sides must be straight.

6. Are the thicker sides parallel?

a)  b)  c)   d)

_____   _____   _____   _____

G3-7 More Special Quadrilaterals

A **parallelogram** is a quadrilateral with 2 pairs of parallel sides.

A **trapezoid** is a quadrilateral with only I pair of parallel sides.

1. Write ✓ beside the name that matches the shape.

a)

b)

c)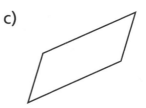

| □ Trapezoid | □ Trapezoid | □ Trapezoid |
| □ Parallelogram | □ Parallelogram | □ Parallelogram |

2. Mark parallel sides with arrows. Label the shape as a "trapezoid," "parallelogram," or "neither."

a)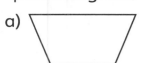
_____

b)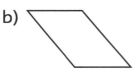
_____

c)
_____

d)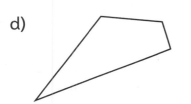
_____

e)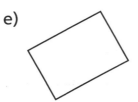
_____

f)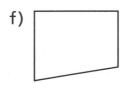
_____

g)
_____

h)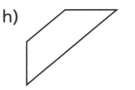
_____

i)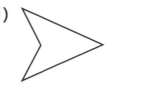
_____

3. Does the name match the shape? Write ✓ or ✗.

a)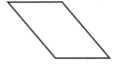

☒ Rectangle

✓ Parallelogram

b)

☐ Rectangle

☐ Parallelogram

c)

☐ Rectangle

☐ Parallelogram

d)

☐ Rectangle

☐ Parallelogram

e)

☐ Rectangle

☐ Parallelogram

f)

☐ Rectangle

☐ Parallelogram

4. Does the name match the shape? Write ✓ or ✗.

a)

☒ Rhombus

✓ Parallelogram

b)

☐ Rhombus

☐ Parallelogram

c)

☐ Rhombus

☐ Parallelogram

d)

☐ Rhombus

☐ Parallelogram

e)

☐ Rhombus

☐ Parallelogram

f)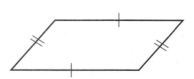

☐ Rhombus

☐ Parallelogram

Geometry 3-7

1. Compare the two shapes by completing the table.

			Same?
Number of sides	4	4	yes
Number of right angles	4	4	
Number of pairs of parallel sides	2	2	
Are all sides equal?	yes	no	

2. Compare the two shapes by completing the table.

			Same?
Number of sides			
Number of right angles			
Number of pairs of parallel sides			
Are all sides equal?			

3. Compare the two shapes by completing the table.

			Same?
Number of sides			
Number of right angles			
Number of pairs of parallel sides			
Are all sides equal?			

4. Compare the two shapes by completing the table.

			Same?
Number of sides			
Number of vertices			
Number of right angles			
Number of pairs of parallel sides			
Are all sides equal?			

5. Compare the two shapes by completing the table.

			Same?
Number of sides			
Number of vertices			
Number of right angles			
Number of pairs of parallel sides			
Are all sides equal?			

6. The shapes in Questions I, 2, and 3 have the same number of sides.

Do they have the same number of vertices? _____

BONUS ▶ Make a table to compare the two shapes.

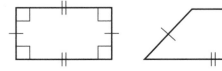

G3-9 Polygons (Advanced)

1. a) Complete the table using the shapes below.
   Write "yes" or "no" in each column.

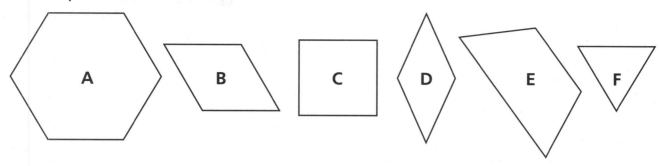

Shape	Quadrilateral	All sides equal	Has right angles	Has exactly 2 pairs of parallel sides
A				
B				
C				
D				
E				
F				

   b) What 3 shapes in part a) are rhombuses? _____

   c) What quadrilateral is not a parallelogram? _____

2. Use pattern blocks to build a shape that matches the description.
   Draw a picture that shows the blocks you used in the shape you built.

   a) Use some of one type of rhombus to make a hexagon.

   b) Use two different types of blocks together to make a trapezoid.

   c) Use a trapezoid and another type of block to make a parallelogram.

   d) Use two blocks to make a rhombus.

   BONUS ▶ Use a hexagon and some other blocks to make a quadrilateral.

3. Describe how the shapes are the same and how they are different. You should include:

- the number of vertices
- the number of sides
- the number of right angles
- the number of pairs of parallel sides
- if all sides are equal

rhombus   trapezoid

4. Describe the shape. You should include:

- the number of sides
- the number of vertices
- the number of pairs of parallel sides
- if all sides are equal
- the number of right angles
- the best possible name for the shape

a)

b)

c)

5. Name the polygon based on the description.

a) I have 4 equal sides. All of my angles are right angles.

b) I have 5 sides and 5 vertices.

c) I am a quadrilateral with 1 pair of parallel sides.

d) I am a quadrilateral with 4 equal sides. None of my angles are right angles.

e) I have 6 sides and 6 vertices.

f) I am a quadrilateral. I have 2 short equal sides and 2 long equal sides. None of my angles are right angles.

In a **fraction**, there are **equal parts** in the whole.

2 equal parts | ← Each part is one half.

3 equal parts | ← one third

4 equal parts | ← one fourth

6 equal parts | ← one sixth

8 equal parts | ← one eighth

I. Use **paper-folding** to fill in the blanks.

a)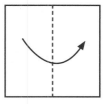

___2___ equal parts

Each part is ___one___ ___half___ .

b)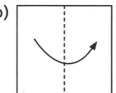

unfolded

_____ equal parts

Each part is _____ _____ .

c)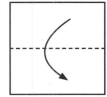

_____ equal parts

Each part is _____ _____ .

d)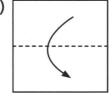

_____ equal parts

Each part is _____ _____ .

e)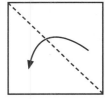

_____ equal parts

Each part is _____ _____ .

f)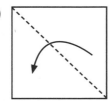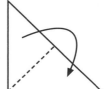

_____ equal parts

Each part is _____ _____ .

2. Use paper-folding to fill in the blanks.

a)

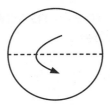

_____ equal parts

Each part is _____ _____.

b)

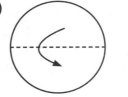

_____ equal parts

Each part is _____ _____.

c)

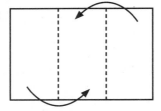

_____ equal parts

Each part is _____ _____.

d)

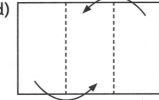

_____ equal parts

Each part is _____ _____.

e)

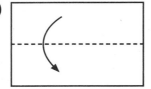

_____ equal parts

Each part is _____ _____.

f)

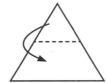

_____ equal parts

Each part is _____ _____.

BONUS ▶

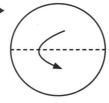 

_____ equal parts

Each part is _____ _____.

3. Kyle thinks that each part in the picture is one sixth of the whole. Is he correct? Explain.

NF3-2 Unit Fractions

There are 4 equal parts.

Each part is one fourth.

One fourth is a fraction.

one fourth or $\frac{1}{4}$

You can write fractions with words or numbers.

← number of parts shaded
← number of parts in the whole

I. Write the fraction for the equal parts with words and with numbers.

a)

___8___ equal parts

Each part is

___one___ ___eighth___ or $\boxed{\frac{1}{8}}$.

b)

_____ equal parts

Each part is

_____ _____ or $\boxed{}$.

c)

_____ equal parts

Each part is

_____ _____ or $\boxed{}$.

d)

_____ equal parts

Each part is

_____ _____ or $\boxed{}$.

e)

_____ equal parts

Each part is

_____ _____ or $\boxed{}$.

f)

_____ equal parts

Each part is

_____ _____ or $\boxed{}$.

A **unit fraction** has only 1 equal part shaded. 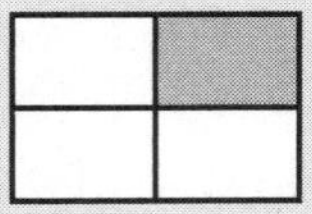 $\frac{1}{4}$

2. Write the unit fraction shown by the shaded part of the picture.

a) $\frac{1}{4}$

b) 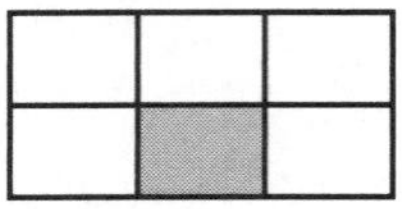 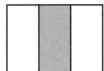 ☐

c) 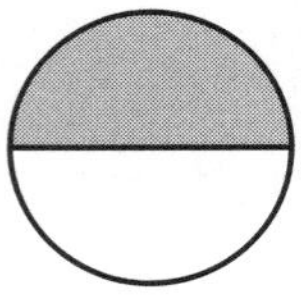 ☐

d) 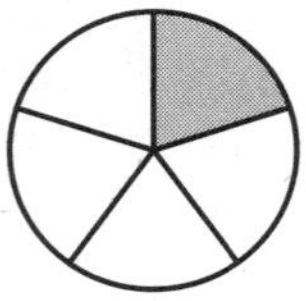 ☐

e)  ☐

f) 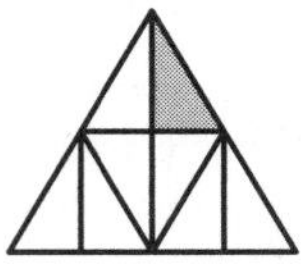 ☐

3. Shade the unit fraction.

a) $\frac{1}{5}$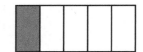

b) $\frac{1}{2}$

c) $\frac{1}{4}$

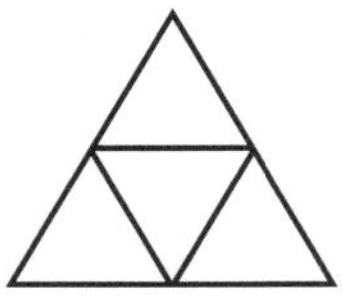

d) $\frac{1}{10}$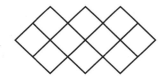

e) $\frac{1}{3}$

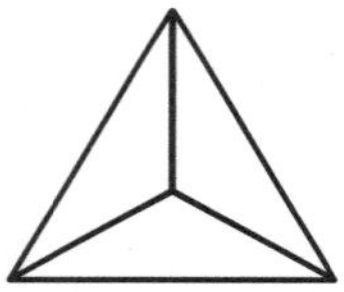

f) $\frac{1}{6}$

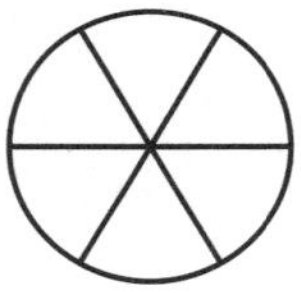

4. Circle the unit fractions.

$\frac{2}{3}$ $\left(\frac{1}{4}\right)$ $\frac{1}{8}$ $\frac{4}{7}$ $\frac{1}{5}$ $\frac{9}{10}$ $\frac{1}{6}$ $\frac{2}{9}$

5. Circle the pictures that do not show one fourth.

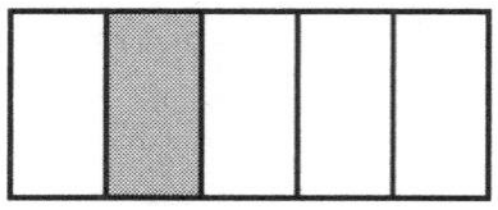

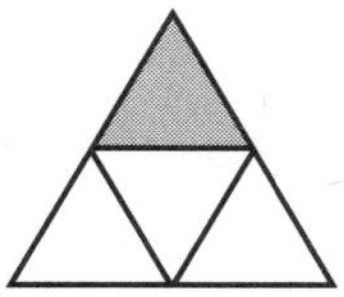

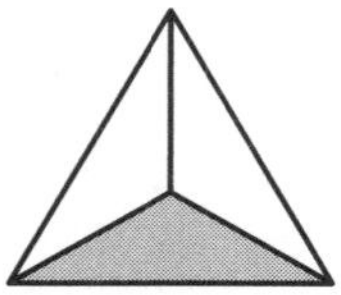

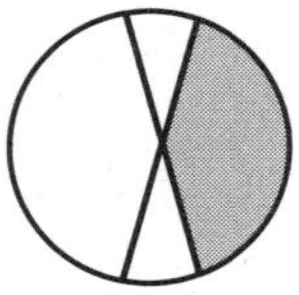

BONUS ▶ Imagine folding a piece of paper to show one fourth.
Draw lines to show the folds. Shade one fourth.

There are 4 equal parts. You can write the fraction as $\frac{3}{4}$.
3 parts are shaded.

$\frac{3}{4}$ ← The **numerator** tells you 3 parts are shaded.

← The **denominator** tells you 4 parts are in the whole.

I. Count the number of shaded parts and the number of equal parts in the picture. Then write the fraction shown by the shaded parts.

a)
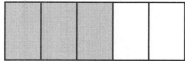

___3___ shaded parts

___5___ equal parts

The fraction is $\boxed{\frac{3}{5}}$.

b)

_____ shaded parts

_____ equal parts

The fraction is $\boxed{}$.

c)
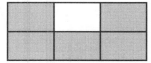

_____ shaded parts

_____ equal parts

The fraction is $\boxed{}$.

d)

_____ shaded parts

_____ equal parts

The fraction is $\boxed{}$.

2. Write the fraction shown by the shaded part or parts.

a)
 $\boxed{\frac{2}{5}}$

b)
 $\boxed{}$

c)
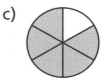 $\boxed{}$

d)
 $\boxed{}$

e)
 $\boxed{}$

f)
 $\boxed{}$

3. Shade parts to show the fraction.

a) $\frac{3}{4}$

b) $\frac{2}{3}$

c) $\frac{1}{5}$

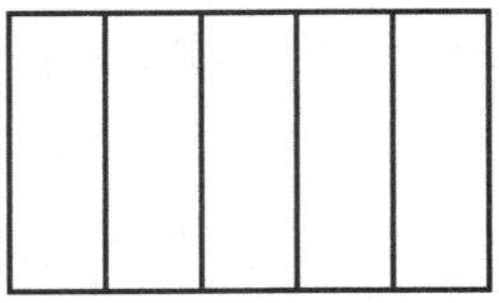

d) $\frac{7}{8}$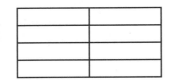

e) $\frac{5}{6}$

f) $\frac{2}{2}$

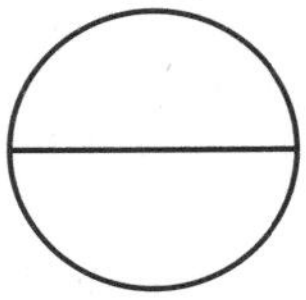

4. Write a fraction for the parts that are not shaded.

a)

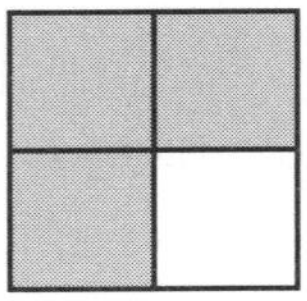

b)

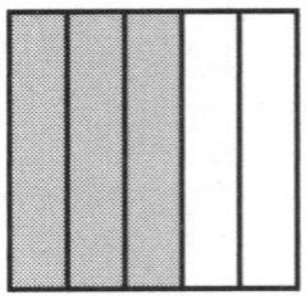

c)

d)

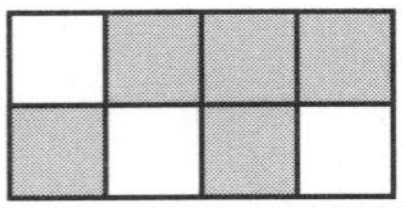

e)

f)

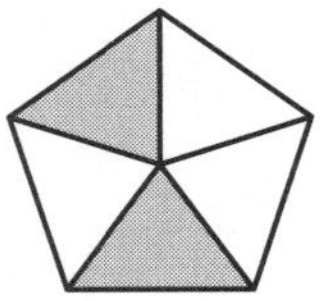

5. Circle the pictures that do not show $\frac{2}{3}$.

 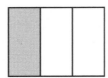

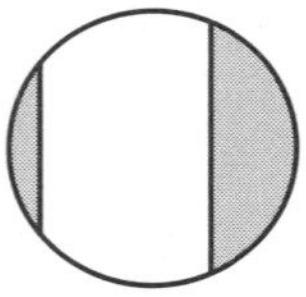

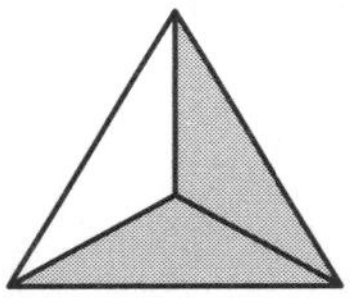

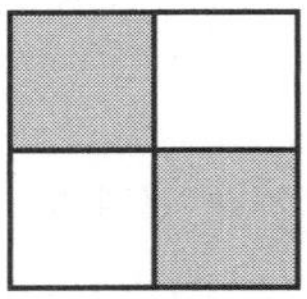

6. For each picture that you circled in Question 5, explain why it does not show $\frac{2}{3}$.

7. You have $\frac{2}{5}$ of a pie.

a) What does the denominator of the fraction tell you?

b) What does the numerator of the fraction tell you?

BONUS ▶ If $\frac{5}{8}$ of a circle is shaded, what fraction of the circle is not shaded?

Hint: Draw a picture.

NF3-4 Fractions and Pattern Blocks

These are **pattern blocks** for four shapes.

triangle   rhombus   trapezoid   hexagon

1. a) Which shape has six sides? _____

b) Which shape has three sides? _____

c) Which shape has only one pair of parallel sides? _____

d) Which shape has two pairs of parallel sides? _____

2. a) Connect the dots with a line.
How many triangles cover the rhombus? _____

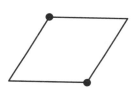

b) Connect each pair of dots with a line.
How many triangles cover the trapezoid? _____

c) Draw lines from the point in the center of the hexagon to each vertex.

How many triangles cover the hexagon? _____

3. What fraction of the pattern block is the shaded triangle?

a)

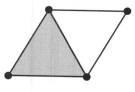

$\dfrac{1}{2}$

b)

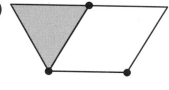

c)

4. a) What fraction of the hexagon is the trapezoid?

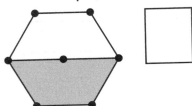

b) What fraction of the hexagon is the rhombus?

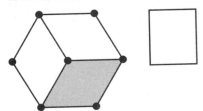

5. What fraction of the picture is shaded?

a)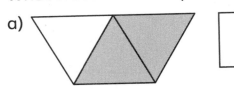

b)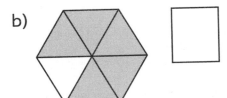

c)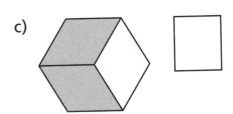

d)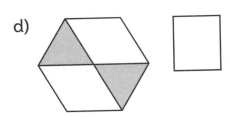

6. What fraction of the picture is shaded?

a)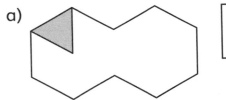

b)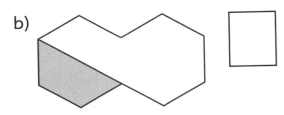

c)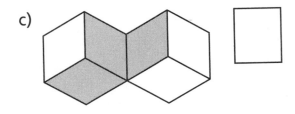

d)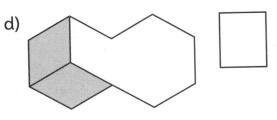

BONUS ▶

e)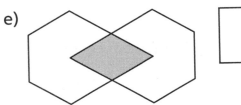

f)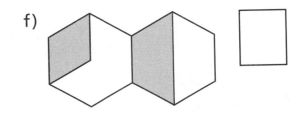

Number and Operations—Fractions 3-4

I. Shade one half of the shape in two different ways.

a)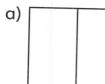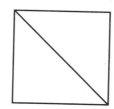

b)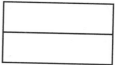

c)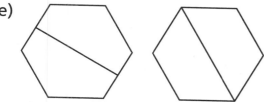

d)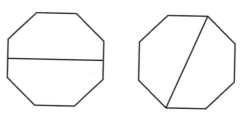

e)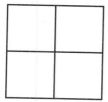

f)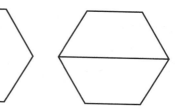

2. Write "yes" or "no" to answer the question for each part in Question I.

a) Are the fractions the same?

b) Do the equal parts look the same?

3. Shade one fourth of the shape in different ways.

a)

b)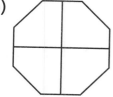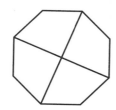

4. Write "yes" or "no" to answer the question for each part in Question 3.

a) Are the fractions the same?

b) Do the equal parts look the same?

5. Add a line to the picture to make 4 equal parts.

a)

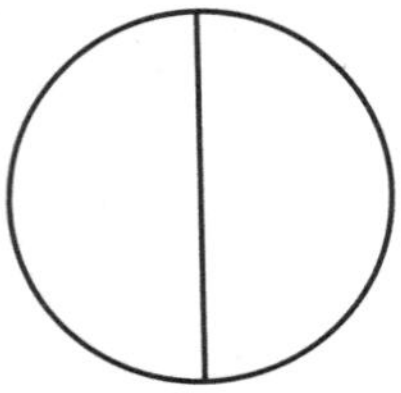

b)

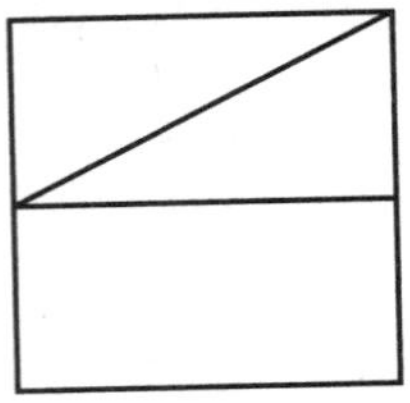

BONUS ▶

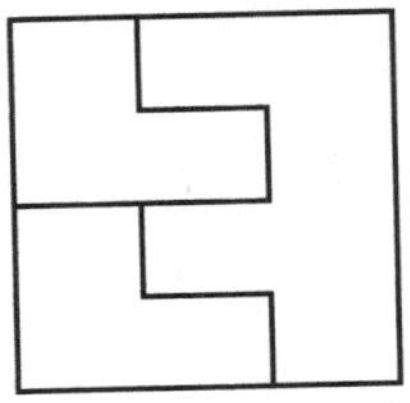

6. Add a line to the picture to make 6 equal parts.

a)

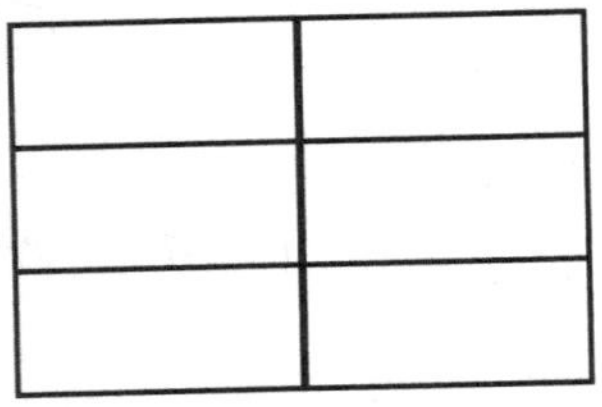

b)

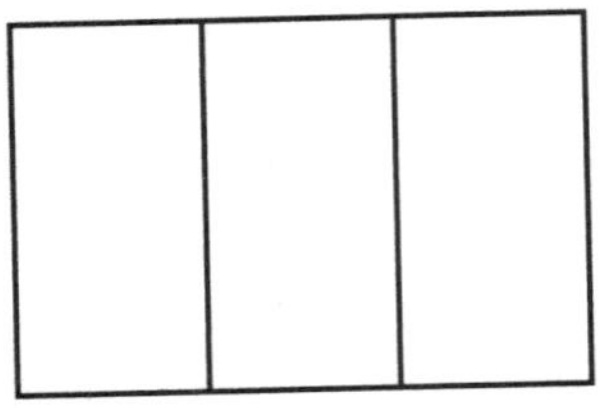

c)

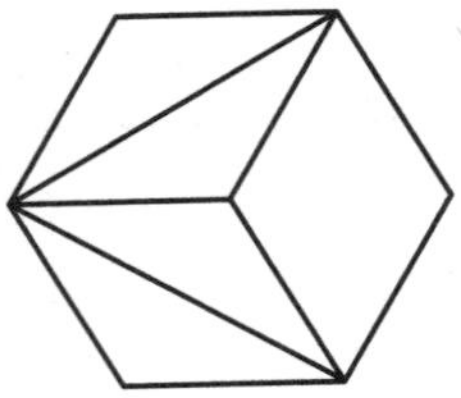

d)

7. John must shade in one fifth of the big square.

Is his answer correct? _____

Explain. _____

_____

_____

_____

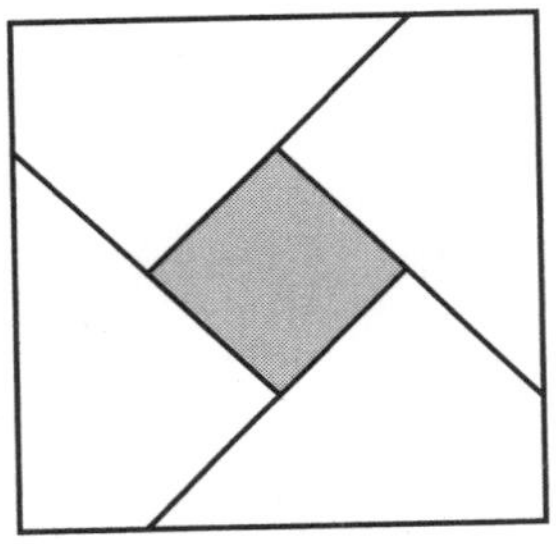

BONUS ▶ Show two different ways to divide a rectangle into 8 equal rectangles.

NF3-6 Different Shapes, Same Fractions

1. Draw a line to create 2 equal parts. Then shade $\frac{1}{2}$ of the whole.

a)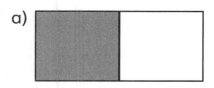

b)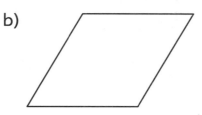

c)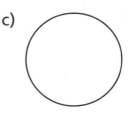

d)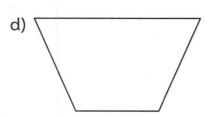

e)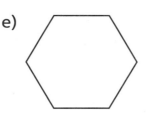

BONUS ▶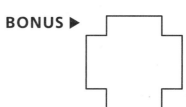

2. Draw a line to create 3 equal parts. Then shade $\frac{2}{3}$ of the whole.

a)

b)

c)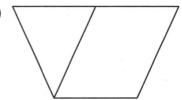

d)

e)

BONUS ▶

3. Draw a line to create 4 equal parts. Then shade $\frac{3}{4}$ of the whole.

a)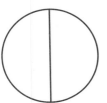

b)

c)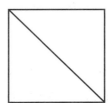

d)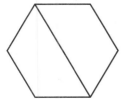

e)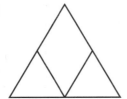

BONUS ▶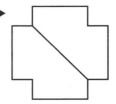

4. One half of a shape is shaded. Outline the whole shape.

a)

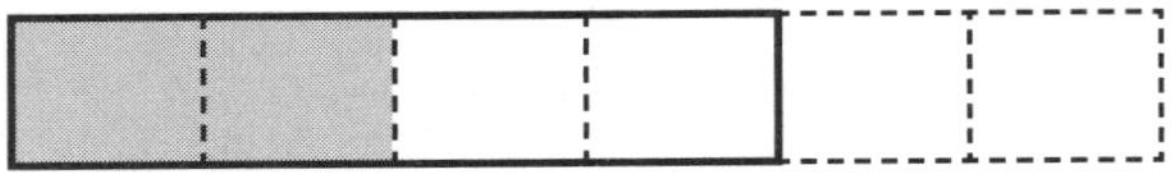

b)

c)

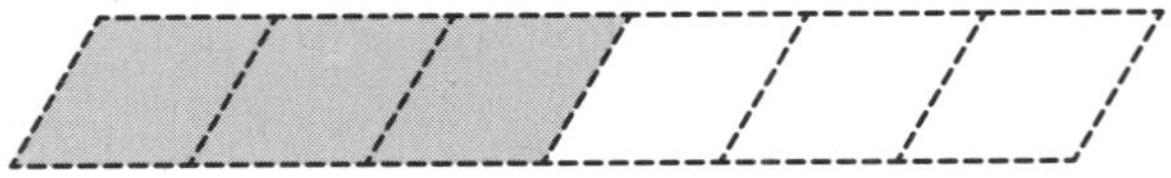

d)

e)

f)

g)

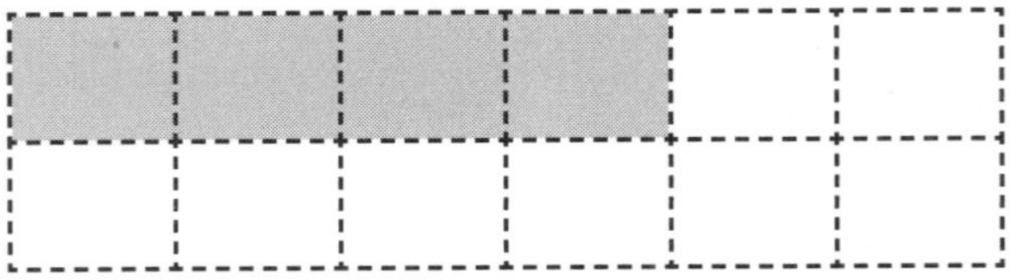

h)

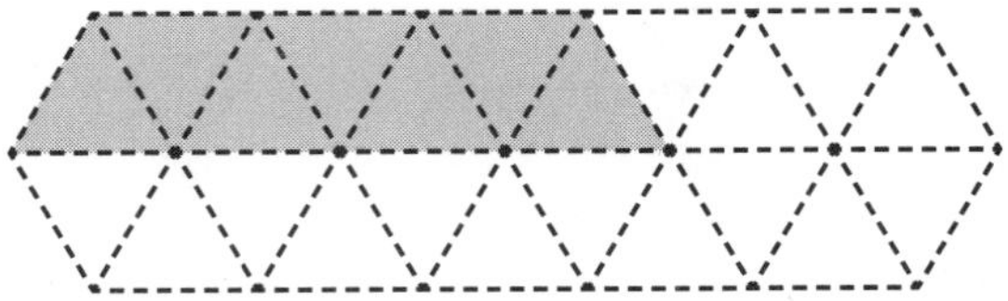

5. One third of a shape is shaded. Outline the whole shape.

a)

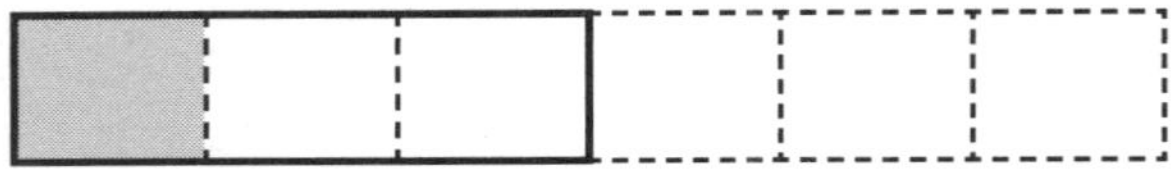

b)

c)

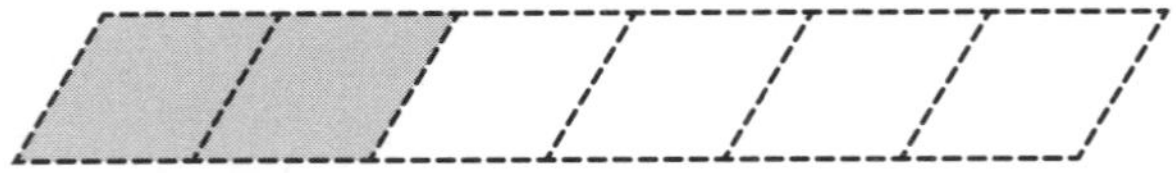

d)

e)

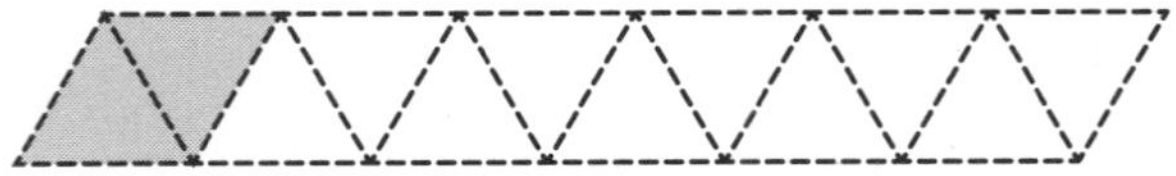

f)

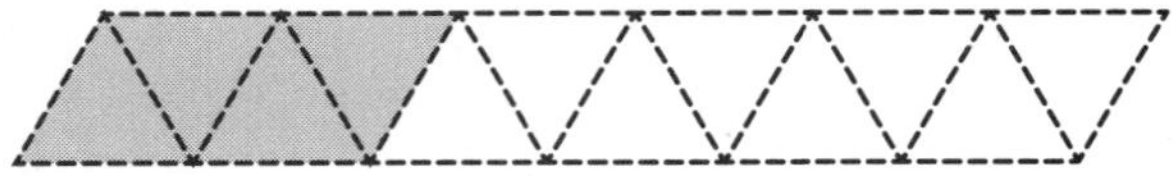

g)

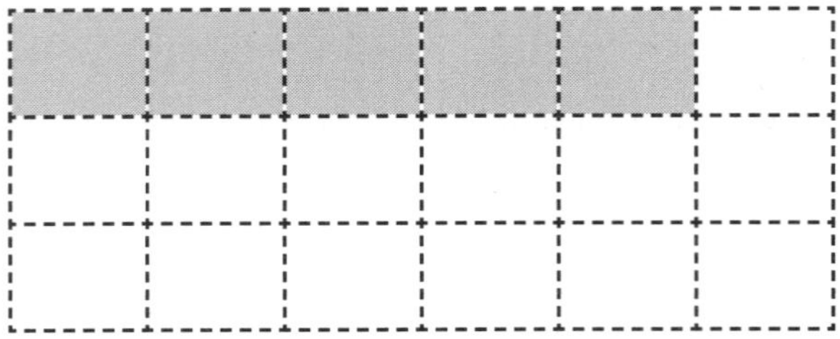

h)

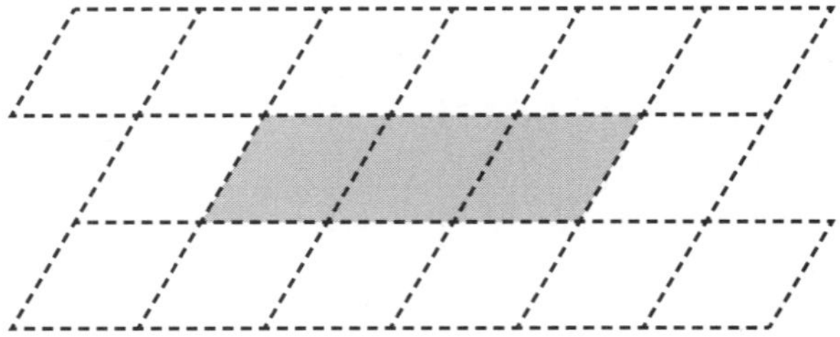

BONUS ▶ One fourth of a shape is shaded. Outline the whole shape.

NF3-7 Comparing Fractions (Introduction)

1. Shade the fraction of the strip.

a) 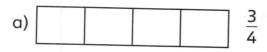 $\frac{3}{4}$

b)  $\frac{2}{3}$

c)  $\frac{2}{5}$

d)  $\frac{7}{8}$

2. Which strip has more shaded? Circle the greater fraction.

a) 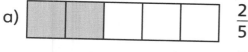 $\frac{2}{5}$

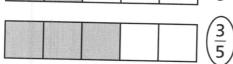 $\left(\frac{3}{5}\right)$

b) 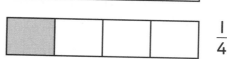 $\frac{3}{4}$

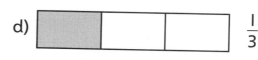 $\frac{1}{4}$

c) 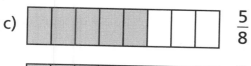 $\frac{5}{8}$

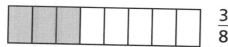 $\frac{3}{8}$

d)  $\frac{1}{3}$

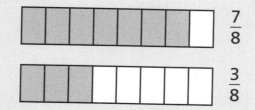 $\frac{2}{3}$

$\frac{7}{8}$ is greater than $\frac{3}{8}$ because more of the whole is shaded.

$\frac{7}{8}$

$\frac{3}{8}$

3. Shade the fractions of the strips. Then circle the greater fraction.

a) 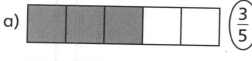 $\left(\frac{3}{5}\right)$

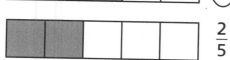 $\frac{2}{5}$

b)  $\frac{3}{4}$

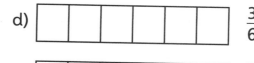 $\frac{1}{4}$

c) 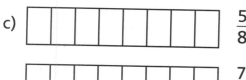 $\frac{5}{8}$

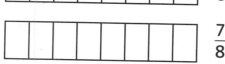 $\frac{7}{8}$

d) 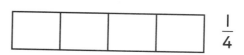 $\frac{3}{6}$

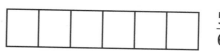 $\frac{5}{6}$

4. Shade the fractions of the strips. Then circle the smaller fraction.

a) $\frac{2}{3}$

$\frac{1}{3}$

b) $\frac{5}{6}$

$\frac{6}{6}$

c) $\frac{3}{7}$

$\frac{6}{7}$

d) $\frac{0}{4}$

$\frac{1}{4}$

"5 is greater than 3" is written as 5 > 3.   "3 is less than 5" is written as 3 < 5.

5. Circle the greater fraction. Then use the correct sign (> or <) to compare the fractions.

a) $\frac{2}{5}$

$\left(\frac{3}{5}\right)$

$\frac{2}{5}$ $\boxed{<}$ $\frac{3}{5}$

b) $\frac{3}{4}$

$\frac{1}{4}$

$\frac{3}{4}$ $\square$ $\frac{1}{4}$

c) $\frac{5}{8}$

$\frac{3}{8}$

$\frac{5}{8}$ $\square$ $\frac{3}{8}$

d) $\frac{3}{6}$

$\frac{5}{6}$

$\frac{3}{6}$ $\square$ $\frac{5}{6}$

6. Nancy looked at the pictures and said that $\frac{1}{3} > \frac{2}{3}$. Explain her mistake.

$\frac{1}{3}$

$\frac{2}{3}$

Number and Operations—Fractions 3-7

NF3-8 Equal Parts and Models of Fractions

I. Use the centimeter ruler to divide the line into equal parts.
Mark with ticks on the line.

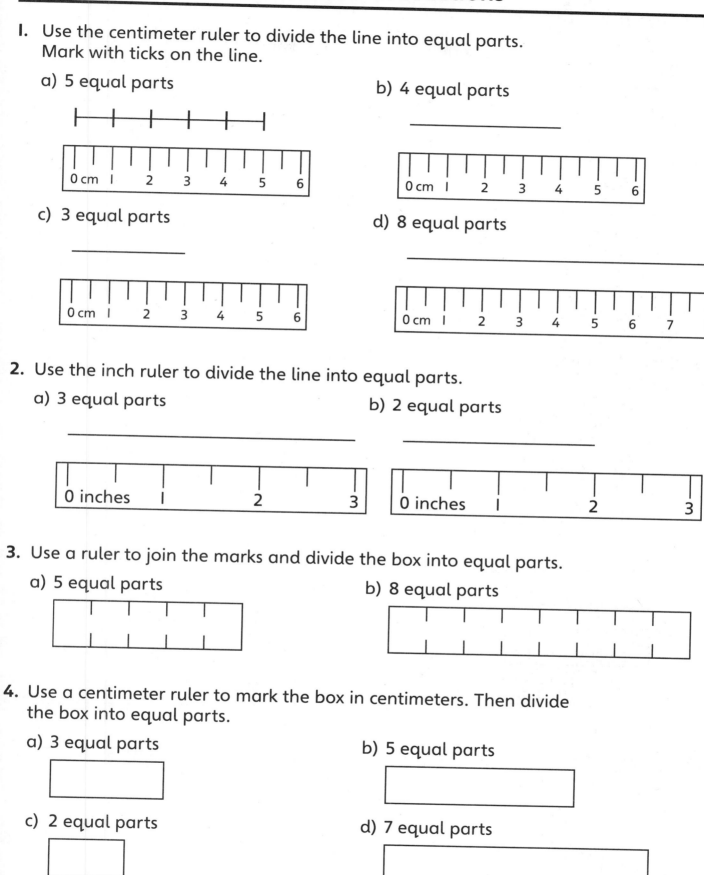

a) 5 equal parts

b) 4 equal parts

c) 3 equal parts

d) 8 equal parts

2. Use the inch ruler to divide the line into equal parts.

a) 3 equal parts

b) 2 equal parts

3. Use a ruler to join the marks and divide the box into equal parts.

a) 5 equal parts

b) 8 equal parts

4. Use a centimeter ruler to mark the box in centimeters. Then divide the box into equal parts.

a) 3 equal parts

b) 5 equal parts

c) 2 equal parts

d) 7 equal parts

You can use a piece of paper to divide the rectangle into equal parts. For example, divide the rectangle into 4 equal parts.

Step 1:   **Step 2:**   **Step 3:**   **Step 4:**

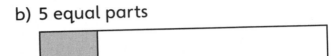

5. Use a piece of paper to divide the rectangle into equal parts.

a) 3 equal parts

b) 5 equal parts

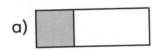

6. Use a ruler or a piece of paper to find what fraction of the rectangle is shaded.

a)

$\dfrac{1}{3}$

b)

c)

d)

7. Use the ruler to draw the rest of the whole shape. Shade the fraction named.

a) $\dfrac{3}{4}$
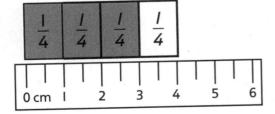

b) $\dfrac{4}{5}$
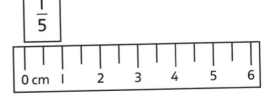

c) $\dfrac{2}{3}$
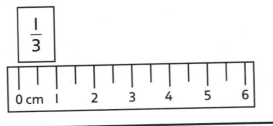

d) $\dfrac{3}{6}$
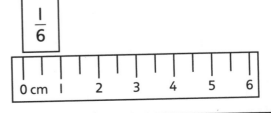

You can also use number lines to show fractions.

$\frac{2}{3}$ of the strip is shaded.

$\frac{2}{3}$ of the number line from 0 to 1 is shaded.

1. Write what fraction of the strip is shaded. Then label the fraction on the number line.

a)
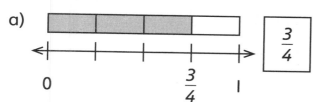
$\frac{3}{4}$

b)
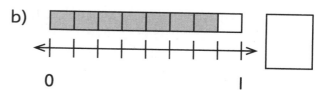

c)
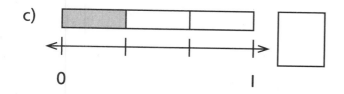

d)
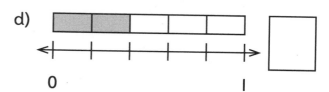

e)
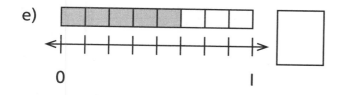

f)
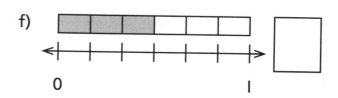

2. Shade the fraction of the strip that shows the fraction on the number line.

a)
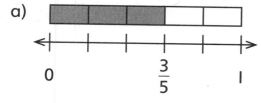

b)
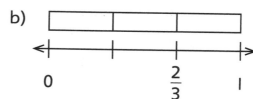

c)
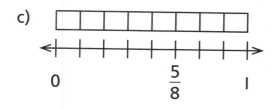

d)
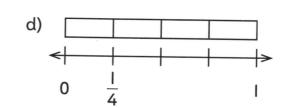

You can label a number line with fractions.

$\frac{0}{3}$

$\frac{0}{3}$ $\frac{1}{3}$

$\frac{0}{3}$ $\frac{1}{3}$ $\frac{2}{3}$

$\frac{0}{3}$ $\frac{1}{3}$ $\frac{2}{3}$ $\frac{3}{3}$

There are 3 equal parts in the whole.

3. Count the number of parts in the whole. Then label all the fractions on the number line.

a) 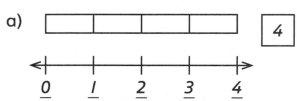   4

$\frac{0}{4}$ $\frac{1}{4}$ $\frac{2}{4}$ $\frac{3}{4}$ $\frac{4}{4}$

b)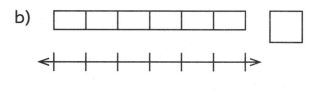

c)

d)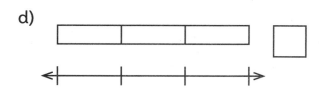

e)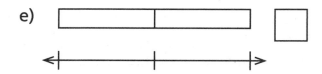

f)

BONUS ▶ Each inch on a six-inch ruler needs to be marked with fourths.

How many fourths will be marked on the entire ruler? _____
Mark them.

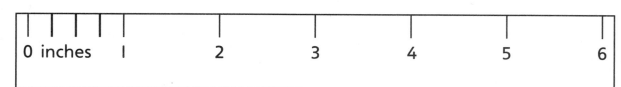

1. The dot on the number line marks a fraction. Count the equal parts and label the dot.

a)

0                    $\frac{3}{4}$ 1

b)

0   1

c)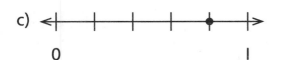

0   1

d)

0   1

e)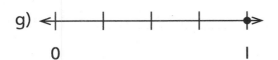

0   1

f)

0   1

g)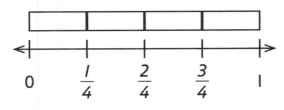

0   1

h)

0   1

2. Fold paper to mark and label the fractions on the number line.

a) fourths

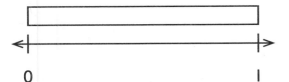

0    $\frac{1}{4}$ $\frac{2}{4}$ $\frac{3}{4}$ 1

b) halves

0   1

c) thirds

0   1

d) eighths

0   1

3. Divide the number line from 0 to 1 into equal parts. Then mark the fraction.

a) 3 equal parts and mark $\frac{2}{3}$

0      $\frac{2}{3}$ 1

b) 2 equal parts and mark $\frac{1}{2}$

0   1

c) 4 equal parts and mark $\frac{1}{4}$

0   1

d) 8 equal parts and mark $\frac{5}{8}$

0   1

4. Circle the larger fraction on the number line.

a)

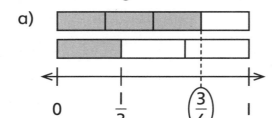

0      $\frac{1}{3}$ $\left(\frac{3}{4}\right)$ 1

b)

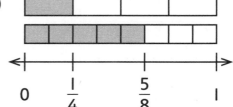

0      $\frac{1}{4}$ $\frac{5}{8}$ 1

c)

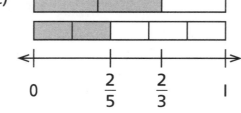

0      $\frac{2}{5}$ $\frac{2}{3}$ 1

d)

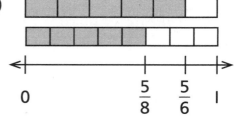

0      $\frac{5}{8}$ $\frac{5}{6}$ 1

> You can use number lines to compare fractions. $\frac{3}{4}$ is farther to the right on the number line than $\frac{1}{3}$, so $\frac{3}{4}$ is greater than $\frac{1}{3}$. You write $\frac{3}{4} > \frac{1}{3}$.

5. Several fractions with different denominators have been marked on the number line.

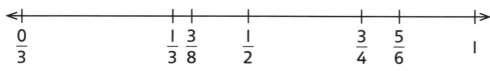

$\frac{0}{3}$ $\frac{1}{3}$ $\frac{3}{8}$ $\frac{1}{2}$ $\frac{3}{4}$ $\frac{5}{6}$ 1

Write < (less than) or > (greater than) to compare fractions.

a) $\frac{1}{3} \boxed{} \frac{1}{2}$ b) $\frac{5}{6} \boxed{} \frac{3}{8}$ c) $\frac{3}{4} \boxed{} \frac{3}{8}$ d) $\frac{1}{2} \boxed{} \frac{5}{6}$

NF3-II Equivalent Fractions

Two thirds equals four sixths because the same amount of the whole is shaded.

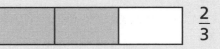

$\frac{2}{3}$

$\frac{2}{3}$ and $\frac{4}{6}$ are **equivalent fractions**.

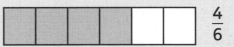

$\frac{4}{6}$

I. Write the equivalent fraction.

a)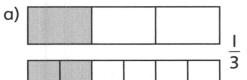

$\frac{1}{3} = \boxed{}$

b)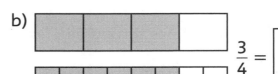

$\frac{3}{4} = \boxed{}$

c)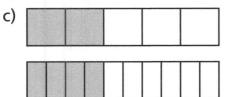

$\frac{2}{5} = \boxed{}$

d)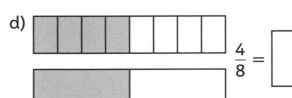

$\frac{4}{8} = \boxed{}$

2. Use dots to mark the equivalent fractions on the number line.

a)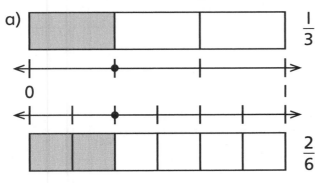

$\frac{1}{3}$

$\frac{2}{6}$

b)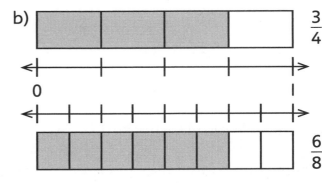

$\frac{3}{4}$

$\frac{6}{8}$

c)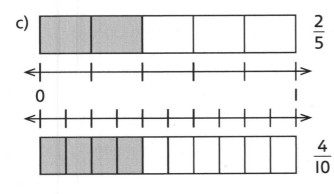

$\frac{2}{5}$

$\frac{4}{10}$

d)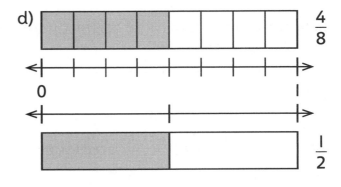

$\frac{4}{8}$

$\frac{1}{2}$

Two fractions are equivalent if you mark them on a number line at the same place.

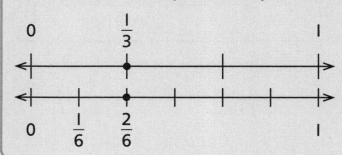

$\frac{1}{3}$ and $\frac{2}{6}$ are equivalent fractions.

You write $\frac{1}{3} = \frac{2}{6}$.

3. Use the number lines to find equivalent fractions.

a)

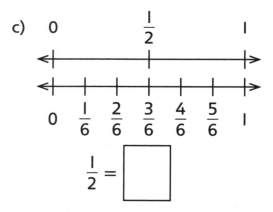

$$\frac{1}{3} = \boxed{} \qquad \frac{2}{3} = \boxed{}$$

b)

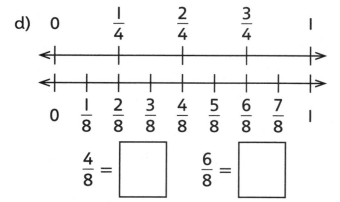

$$\frac{1}{4} = \boxed{} \qquad \frac{3}{4} = \boxed{}$$

c)

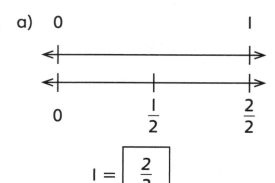

$$\frac{1}{2} = \boxed{}$$

d)

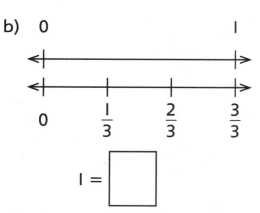

$$\frac{4}{8} = \boxed{} \qquad \frac{6}{8} = \boxed{}$$

4. Use the number lines to write an equivalent fraction.

a)

0   1

0      $\frac{1}{2}$ $\frac{2}{2}$

$$1 = \boxed{\frac{2}{2}}$$

b)

0   1

0    $\frac{1}{3}$ $\frac{2}{3}$ $\frac{3}{3}$

$$1 = \boxed{}$$

5. Use the number lines to write an equivalent fraction.

a)
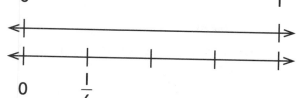

$1 = \boxed{}$

b)
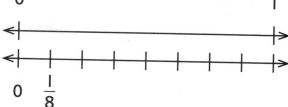

$1 = \boxed{}$

6. Write an equivalent fraction using the given denominator.

a) $1 = \dfrac{}{3}$ b) $1 = \dfrac{}{6}$ c) $1 = \dfrac{}{16}$ **BONUS ▶** $1 = \dfrac{}{199}$

Equivalent fractions name equal parts of the same whole.

 $\dfrac{3}{4}$ Cut each part into 2 new parts $\dfrac{6}{8}$ ← parts shaded ← equal parts   So $\dfrac{3}{4} = \dfrac{6}{8}$.

7. Each part in the whole is cut into 2 equal parts. Write the equivalent fractions.

a)

$\boxed{\dfrac{1}{2}}$ = $\boxed{\dfrac{2}{4}}$

b)
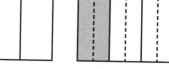 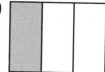

$\boxed{}$ = $\boxed{}$

c)
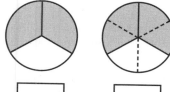

$\boxed{}$ = $\boxed{}$

d)
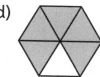

$\boxed{}$ = $\boxed{}$

8. Each part in the whole is cut into 3 equal parts. Write the equivalent fractions.

a)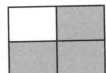

$$\boxed{\dfrac{2}{3}} = \boxed{\dfrac{6}{9}}$$

b)

$$\boxed{} = \boxed{}$$

c)

$$\boxed{} = \boxed{}$$

BONUS ▶

$$\boxed{} = \boxed{}$$

9. Draw lines that divide each part in the whole to show the equivalent fraction.

a)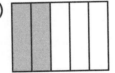

$$\dfrac{2}{5} = \dfrac{4}{10}$$

b)

$$\dfrac{3}{4} = \dfrac{6}{8}$$

c)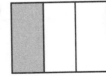

$$\dfrac{1}{3} = \dfrac{3}{9}$$

d)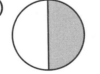

$$\dfrac{1}{2} = \dfrac{3}{6}$$

BONUS ▶ Kate cut each part in the whole into more equal parts and was able to show $\dfrac{2}{3} = \dfrac{10}{15}$. Into how many equal parts did she divide each part of the whole?

Number and Operations—Fractions 3-11

The numbers 0, 1, 2, 3, 4, and so on, are **whole numbers**.

A number line can be labeled with whole numbers or fractions.

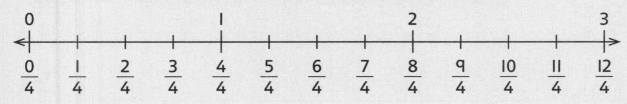

1. Count by the given fraction to label the number line.

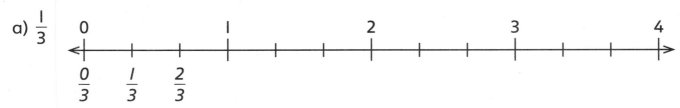

a) $\frac{1}{3}$

b) $\frac{1}{8}$

c) $\frac{1}{2}$

d) $\frac{1}{5}$

2. Use the number lines in Question 1 to find a whole number that is equivalent to the fraction.

a) $\frac{6}{3} = \underline{\quad 2 \quad}$

b) $\frac{15}{5} = \underline{\quad\quad}$

c) $\frac{16}{8} = \underline{\quad\quad}$

d) $\frac{8}{2} = \underline{\quad\quad}$

e) $\frac{12}{2} = \underline{\quad\quad}$

f) $\frac{0}{8} = \underline{\quad\quad}$

g) $\frac{3}{3} = \underline{\quad\quad}$

h) $\frac{5}{5} = \underline{\quad\quad}$

BONUS ▶ What whole number is equivalent to the fraction $\frac{999}{999}$? $\underline{\quad\quad}$

3. Circle the fractions that are equivalent to whole numbers.

a)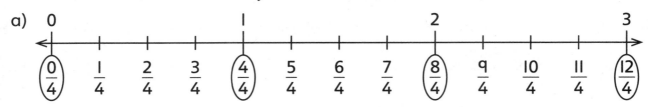

b)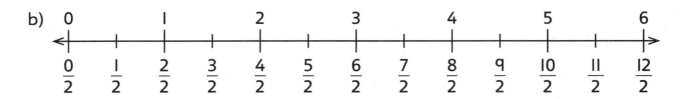

c)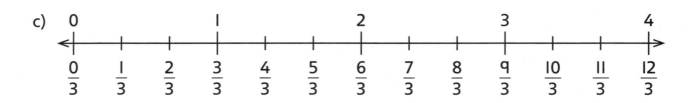

d)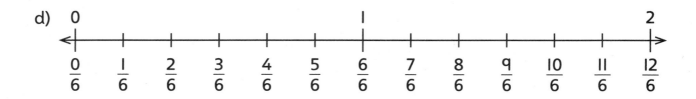

4. Label the whole numbers on the number line.

a) Each mark is one fourth.

b) Each mark is one half.

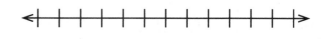

c) Each mark is one third.

d) Each mark is one sixth.

e) Each mark is one eighth.

5. Place a dot where the fraction should go on the number line.

a) $\frac{7}{4}$ 0   1   2

b) $\frac{9}{2}$ 0 1 2 3 4 5 6

c) $\frac{8}{3}$ 0   1   2   3

d) $\frac{11}{8}$ 0   1   2

6. Count the parts in each whole. Then write the fraction to label the dot.

a)   0   1   2   3

    __4__ parts in each whole   fraction $\boxed{\dfrac{7}{4}}$

b)   0   1   2   3   4

    _____ parts in each whole   fraction $\boxed{}$

c)   0   1   2   3   4   5   6

    _____ parts in each whole   fraction $\boxed{}$

d)   0   1   2

    _____ parts in each whole   fraction $\boxed{}$

7. Use the number lines to find equivalent fractions.

a) 0 $\frac{1}{3}$ $\frac{2}{3}$ 1 $\frac{4}{3}$ $\frac{5}{3}$ 2

0   $\frac{1}{6}$ $\frac{2}{6}$ $\frac{3}{6}$ $\frac{4}{6}$ $\frac{5}{6}$ 1 $\frac{7}{6}$ $\frac{8}{6}$ $\frac{9}{6}$ $\frac{10}{6}$ $\frac{11}{6}$ 2

$\frac{2}{3} = \boxed{\frac{4}{6}}$ $\frac{5}{3} = \boxed{}$ $\frac{4}{3} = \boxed{}$ $\frac{2}{6} = \boxed{}$

b) 0 $\frac{1}{2}$ 1 $\frac{3}{2}$ 2 $\frac{5}{2}$ 3 $\frac{7}{2}$ 4

0   $\frac{1}{4}$ $\frac{2}{4}$ $\frac{3}{4}$ 1 $\frac{5}{4}$ $\frac{6}{4}$ $\frac{7}{4}$ 2 $\frac{9}{4}$ $\frac{10}{4}$ $\frac{11}{4}$ 3 $\frac{13}{4}$ $\frac{14}{4}$ $\frac{15}{4}$ 4

$\frac{3}{2} = \boxed{}$ $\frac{5}{2} = \boxed{}$ $\frac{14}{4} = \boxed{}$ $\frac{2}{4} = \boxed{}$

c) 0 $\frac{1}{4}$ $\frac{2}{4}$ $\frac{3}{4}$ 1 $\frac{5}{4}$ $\frac{6}{4}$ $\frac{7}{4}$ 2

0   $\frac{1}{8}$ $\frac{2}{8}$ $\frac{3}{8}$ $\frac{4}{8}$ $\frac{5}{8}$ $\frac{6}{8}$ $\frac{7}{8}$ 1 $\frac{9}{8}$ $\frac{10}{8}$ $\frac{11}{8}$ $\frac{12}{8}$ $\frac{13}{8}$ $\frac{14}{8}$ $\frac{15}{8}$ 2

$\frac{2}{4} = \boxed{}$ $\frac{12}{8} = \boxed{}$ $\frac{14}{8} = \boxed{}$ $\frac{3}{4} = \boxed{}$

BONUS ▶ Use the number lines to find an equivalent fraction.

$\frac{20}{2}$ $\frac{22}{2}$ $\frac{24}{2}$

$\frac{40}{4}$

$\frac{21}{2} = \boxed{}$

NF3-13 Whole Numbers as Fractions

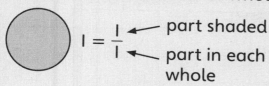

You can write fractions for whole shapes.

$1 = \dfrac{1}{1}$ ← part shaded / part in each whole

$2 = \dfrac{2}{1}$ ← parts shaded / part in each whole

1. Write the whole number as a fraction with the denominator 1.

a) $3 = \boxed{\dfrac{3}{1}}$
   b) $6 = \boxed{}$
   c) $8 = \boxed{}$
   BONUS ▶ $99 = \boxed{}$

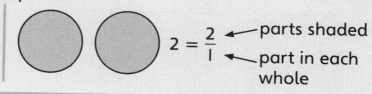

If you draw 2 parts in each whole, the whole number 2 can be written as the fraction $\dfrac{4}{2}$.

$\dfrac{4}{2}$ ← 4 parts shaded / 2 parts in each whole

2. Write the whole number as a fraction with the denominator 2.

a) 3 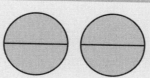 $= \boxed{\dfrac{6}{2}}$

b) 4 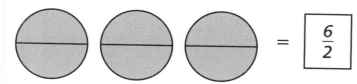 $= \boxed{}$

c) 5 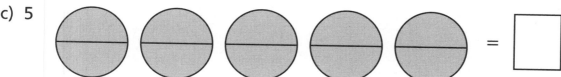 $= \boxed{}$

BONUS ▶ $10 = \boxed{}$

3. Write the whole number as a fraction with the denominator 3.

a) $2 = \dfrac{6}{3}$
   b) $3 = \dfrac{}{3}$
   c) $4 = \dfrac{}{3}$
   BONUS ▶ $10 = \dfrac{}{3}$

4. Write the whole numbers on the number line as fractions.

a)

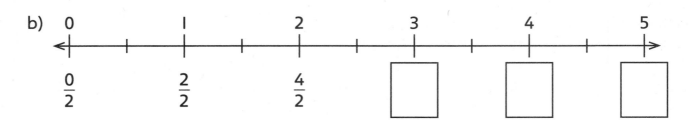

$$\frac{0}{1} \qquad \frac{1}{1} \qquad \frac{2}{1} \qquad \boxed{\frac{3}{1}} \qquad \boxed{\frac{4}{1}} \qquad \boxed{\frac{5}{1}}$$

b)

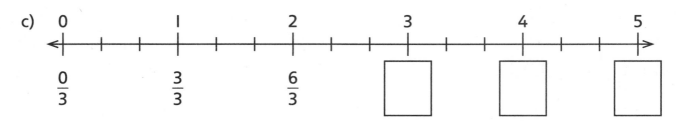

$$\frac{0}{2} \qquad \frac{2}{2} \qquad \frac{4}{2} \qquad \boxed{} \qquad \boxed{} \qquad \boxed{}$$

c)

$$\frac{0}{3} \qquad \frac{3}{3} \qquad \frac{6}{3} \qquad \boxed{} \qquad \boxed{} \qquad \boxed{}$$

d)

$$\frac{0}{4} \qquad \boxed{} \qquad \boxed{} \qquad \boxed{} \qquad \boxed{} \qquad \boxed{}$$

e)

$$\frac{0}{6} \qquad \boxed{} \qquad \boxed{} \qquad \boxed{} \qquad \boxed{} \qquad \boxed{}$$

BONUS ▶

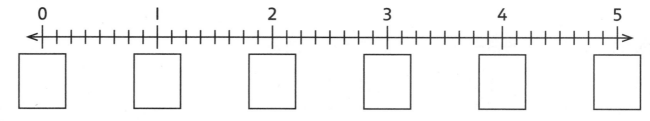

$$\boxed{} \qquad \boxed{} \qquad \boxed{} \qquad \boxed{} \qquad \boxed{} \qquad \boxed{}$$

NF3-14 Mixed Numbers (Advanced)

Helen and her friends cut some pizzas into quarters.

They ate 11 of the quarters or $\frac{11}{4}$ pizzas.

In this fraction, the **numerator** is larger than the **denominator**.

The fraction represents more than one whole.
These kinds of fractions are called **improper fractions**.

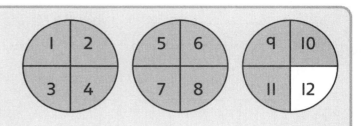

1. Write an improper fraction for the picture.

a) 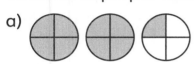 $\frac{9}{4}$

b)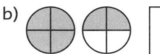

c)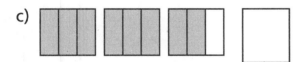

d)

e)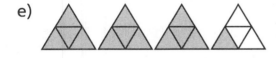

f)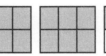

2. Write an improper fraction to label the dot.

a) 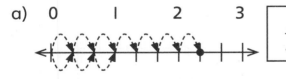 $\frac{7}{3}$

b)

c) 0 1 2 3 4 5 6

d) 0   1   2

BONUS ▶ Write an improper fraction for the picture.

3. Shade one part at a time until the picture shows the given fraction.

a) $\frac{7}{4}$

b) $\frac{10}{3}$

c) $\frac{5}{2}$

d) $\frac{19}{6}$

4. Place a dot on the number line to show the fraction.

a) $\frac{9}{4}$

b) $\frac{7}{2}$

c) $\frac{8}{3}$

d) $\frac{10}{6}$

Helen and her friends ate $\frac{11}{4}$ pizzas.

You can write $\frac{11}{4}$ as $2\frac{3}{4}$.

$2\frac{3}{4}$ is called a **mixed number** because it is a mixture of a whole number and a fraction.

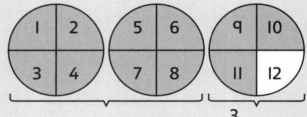

2 whole pizzas + $\frac{3}{4}$ pizza

5. Write the whole number and the fraction. Then write the mixed number.

a)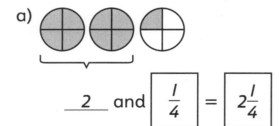

__2__ and $\boxed{\frac{1}{4}}$ = $\boxed{2\frac{1}{4}}$

b)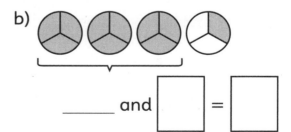

_____ and $\boxed{}$ = $\boxed{}$

c)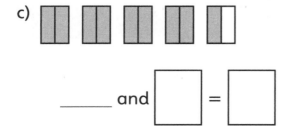

_____ and $\boxed{}$ = $\boxed{}$

d)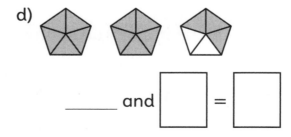

_____ and $\boxed{}$ = $\boxed{}$

Number and Operations—Fractions 3-14

6. Shade to show the mixed number.

a) $1\frac{3}{4}$

b) $3\frac{1}{3}$

c) $2\frac{5}{6}$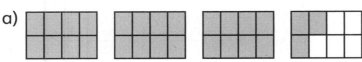

d) $3\frac{7}{9}$

7. Write a mixed number for the dot on the number line.

a) 0   1   2   3   4

$\boxed{2}$ and $\boxed{\frac{1}{3}}$ = $\boxed{2\frac{1}{3}}$

b) 0   1   2   3

$\boxed{}$ and $\boxed{}$ = $\boxed{}$

c) 0 1 2 3 4 5 6

$\boxed{}$ and $\boxed{}$ = $\boxed{}$

d) 0   1   2

$\boxed{}$ and $\boxed{}$ = $\boxed{}$

8. Write an improper fraction and a mixed number for the picture.

	Improper Fraction	Mixed Number
a) 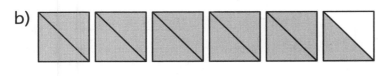	$\boxed{}$	$\boxed{}$
b) 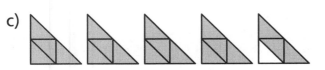	$\boxed{}$	$\boxed{}$
c) 	$\boxed{}$	$\boxed{}$

BONUS ▶ What improper fraction is equal to $10\frac{1}{2}$? _____

> REMINDER ▶ $\frac{2}{3}$ ← The numerator tells you how many parts are shaded
> ← The denominator tells you how many equal parts are in the whole.

1. Write the fraction that is shaded in each shape. Circle the larger fraction.

a) 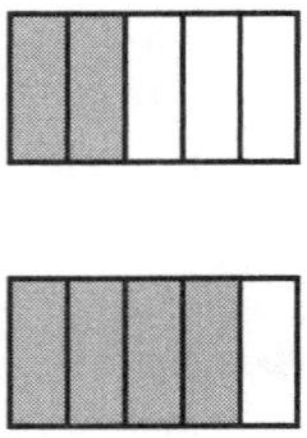 $\frac{2}{5}$

$\left(\frac{4}{5}\right)$

b)

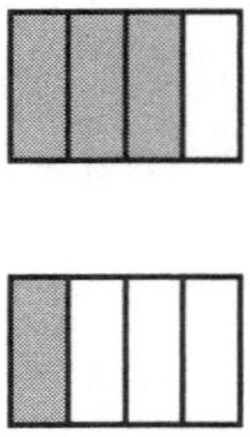

c)

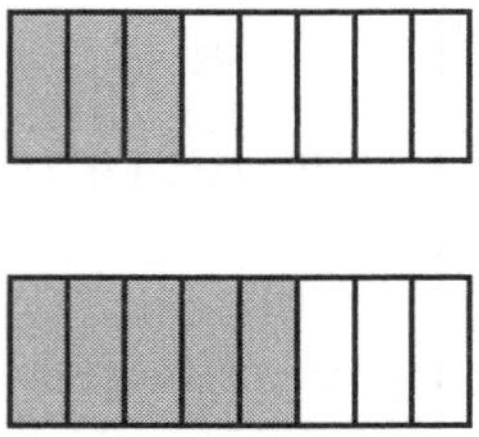

d)

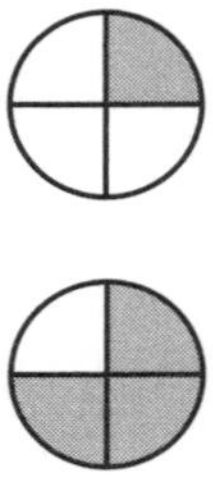

e)

f)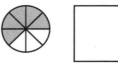

2. Write a fraction for the dot on each number line. Circle the larger fraction.

a) 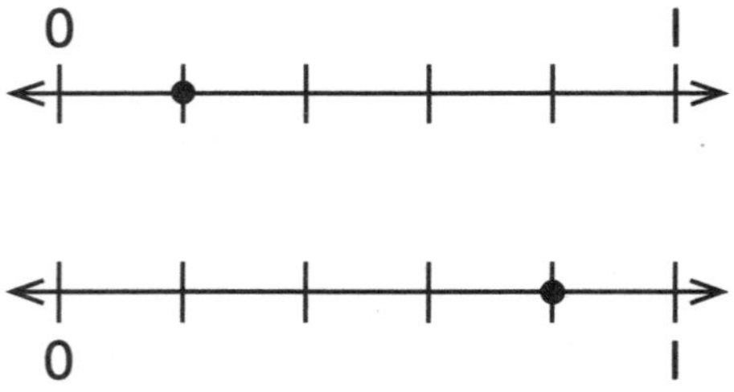 0   1 $\frac{1}{5}$

$\left(\frac{4}{5}\right)$

0   1

b) 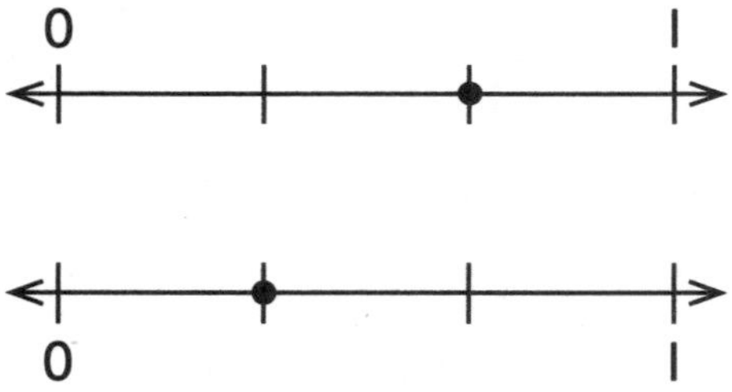 0   1

0   1

c) 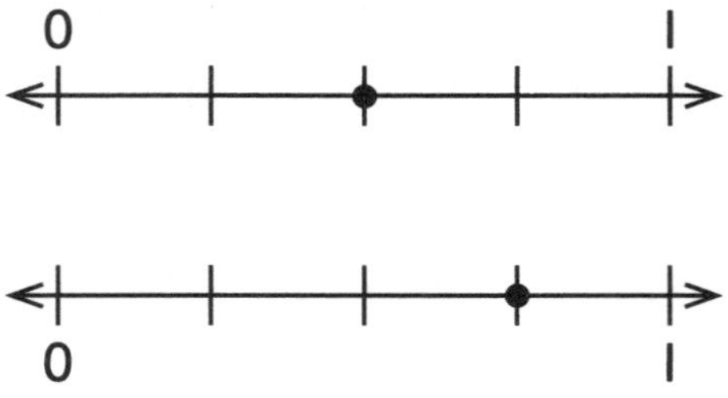 0   1

0   1

d) 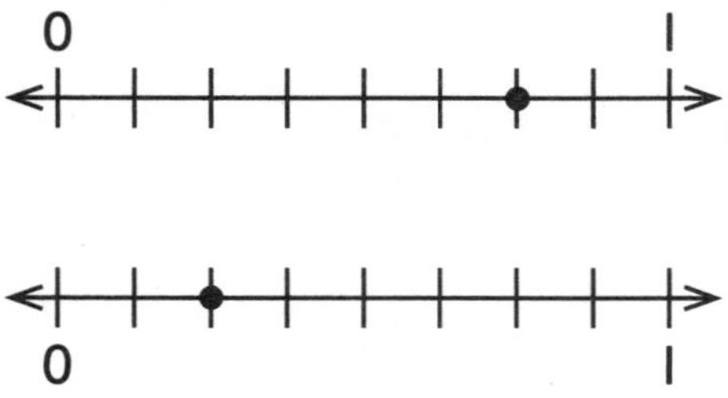 0   1

0   1

3. Circle the correct word.

In each pair of fractions on this page, the   numerators   /   denominators are the same.

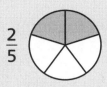

$\dfrac{4}{5}$ ← The denominators → $\dfrac{2}{5}$ are the same.

The numerator of $\dfrac{4}{5}$ is greater than the numerator of $\dfrac{2}{5}$.

More parts are shaded in $\dfrac{4}{5}$ than in $\dfrac{2}{5}$, so $\dfrac{4}{5} > \dfrac{2}{5}$.

4. Compare the numerators. Then circle the larger fraction.

a) $\dfrac{3}{5}$ or $\dfrac{1}{5}$ b) $\dfrac{4}{7}$ or $\dfrac{6}{7}$ c) $\dfrac{7}{8}$ or $\dfrac{1}{8}$ **BONUS ▶** $\dfrac{38}{75}$ or $\dfrac{21}{75}$

5. Compare the numerators and write the fractions in order from largest to smallest.

a) $\dfrac{3}{4}$ $\dfrac{1}{4}$ $\dfrac{2}{4}$

□ > □ > □

b) $\dfrac{5}{8}$ $\dfrac{7}{8}$ $\dfrac{1}{8}$ $\dfrac{8}{8}$

□ > □ > □ > □

6. Compare the numerators and write the fractions in order from smallest to largest.

a) $\dfrac{4}{5}$ $\dfrac{2}{5}$ $\dfrac{5}{5}$

□ < □ < □

b) $\dfrac{7}{16}$ $\dfrac{1}{16}$ $\dfrac{11}{16}$ $\dfrac{14}{16}$

□ < □ < □ < □

7. Write the missing fractions with the denominator 11.

$\dfrac{9}{11} >$ □ $> \dfrac{7}{11} >$ □ $> \dfrac{5}{11}$

8. Write a fraction between the two fractions.

a) $\dfrac{3}{7}$ and $\dfrac{5}{7}$ b) $\dfrac{9}{12}$ and $\dfrac{7}{12}$ c) $\dfrac{10}{16}$ and $\dfrac{12}{16}$ **BONUS ▶** $\dfrac{95}{100}$ and $\dfrac{97}{100}$

NF3-16 Fractions with the Same Numerator

1. Write the fraction that is shaded. Circle the larger fraction.

a)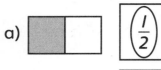

b)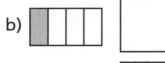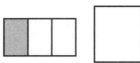

c)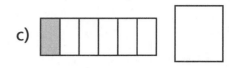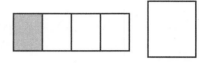

d)

e)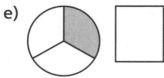

f)

2. Write a fraction for the dot on each number line. Circle the larger fraction.

a)

b)

c)

d)

3. Circle the correct word.

In each pair of fractions on this page, the   numerators / denominators are the same.

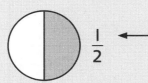 $\frac{1}{2}$ ←——— The numerators ———→ $\frac{1}{4}$
are the same.

The denominator of $\frac{1}{2}$ is smaller than the denominator of $\frac{1}{4}$.

Each equal part in $\frac{1}{2}$ is larger than each equal part in $\frac{1}{4}$, so $\frac{1}{2} > \frac{1}{4}$.

4. Compare the denominators. Then circle the larger fraction.

a) $\frac{1}{4}$ or $\frac{1}{3}$ 　　　　b) $\frac{1}{4}$ or $\frac{1}{8}$ 　　　　c) $\frac{1}{6}$ or $\frac{1}{8}$

d) $\frac{1}{2}$ or $\frac{1}{5}$ 　　　　e) $\frac{1}{3}$ or $\frac{1}{16}$ 　　　　**BONUS ▶** $\frac{1}{8}$ or $\frac{1}{99}$

$\frac{1}{3} > \frac{1}{4}$ 　 $\frac{1}{3}$ →  ← $\frac{1}{3}$ 　 $\frac{1}{4}$ →  ← $\frac{1}{4}$

$\frac{2}{3} > \frac{2}{4}$ because each part in $\frac{2}{3}$ is larger than each part in $\frac{2}{4}$.

5. Compare the denominators. Then circle the larger fraction.

a) $\frac{2}{4}$ or $\frac{2}{5}$ 　　　　b) $\frac{3}{8}$ or $\frac{3}{4}$ 　　　　c) $\frac{5}{8}$ or $\frac{5}{6}$

d) $\frac{2}{6}$ or $\frac{2}{3}$ 　　　　e) $\frac{3}{4}$ or $\frac{3}{16}$ 　　　　**BONUS ▶** $\frac{7}{8}$ or $\frac{7}{88}$

6. Compare the denominators. Then write the fractions in order from largest to smallest.

a) $\frac{1}{4}$ $\frac{1}{2}$ $\frac{1}{3}$ □ > □ > □ 　　　　b) $\frac{1}{8}$ $\frac{1}{6}$ $\frac{1}{2}$ □ > □ > □

c) $\frac{3}{4}$ $\frac{3}{6}$ $\frac{3}{8}$ □ > □ > □ 　　　　d) $\frac{5}{6}$ $\frac{5}{10}$ $\frac{5}{8}$ □ > □ > □

NF3-17 Half Squares

1. Count on by the fraction. Use improper fractions.

a) $\frac{1}{4}$, $\frac{2}{4}$, $\frac{3}{4}$, $\frac{4}{4}$, $\frac{5}{4}$, ☐ , ☐ , ☐ , ☐

b) $\frac{1}{3}$, $\frac{2}{3}$, $\frac{3}{3}$, $\frac{4}{3}$, ☐ , ☐ , ☐ , ☐ , ☐

c) $\frac{1}{2}$, $\frac{2}{2}$, $\frac{3}{2}$, ☐ , ☐ , ☐ , ☐ , ☐

2. Count on by the fraction. Use mixed numbers.

a) $\frac{1}{4}$, $\frac{2}{4}$, $\frac{3}{4}$, $\frac{4}{4}$, $1\frac{1}{4}$, ☐ , ☐ , ☐ , ☐

b) $\frac{1}{3}$, $\frac{2}{3}$, $\frac{3}{3}$, $1\frac{1}{3}$, $1\frac{2}{3}$, ☐ , ☐ , ☐ , ☐

c) $\frac{1}{2}$, $\frac{2}{2}$, $1\frac{1}{2}$, 2, $2\frac{1}{2}$, ☐ , ☐ , ☐ , ☐

Two half squares  cover the
same area as one whole square. ◹
You can circle pairs of half squares to find the area.

Area $= 2\frac{1}{2}$

---

3. Find the total area by circling pairs of half squares.

a)  $1\frac{1}{2}$

b)

c)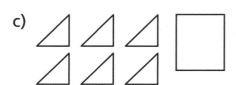

d)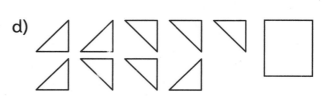

---

4. Count the shaded half squares to find the area. Write the area as a mixed number.

a)  $1\frac{1}{2}$

b)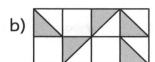

c)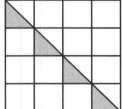

d)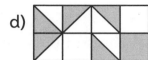

e)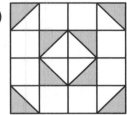

f)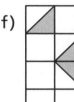

g)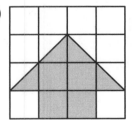

BONUS ▶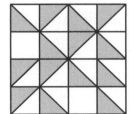

5. Count the shaded half squares to write the total shaded area.

a)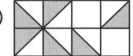

b)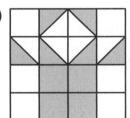

c)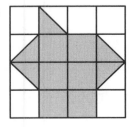

BONUS ▶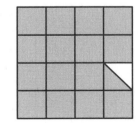

1. John ate $\frac{3}{4}$ of a pie. What fraction of a pie is left? Explain using a picture.

2. Is one half of Picture A the same as one half of Picture B? _____

 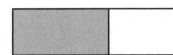

Picture A   Picture B

Explain. _____

_____

3. Shade $\frac{3}{4}$ of the picture.

a)    b)   c)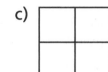

4. Use the pictures to explain why $\frac{1}{2} = \frac{2}{4}$.

5. Use the number lines to explain why $\frac{1}{3} = \frac{2}{6}$.

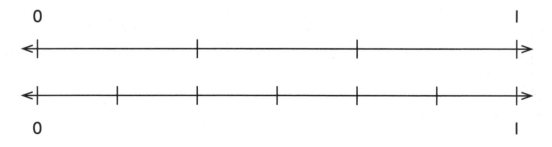

0   1

0   1

6. a) Write an improper fraction for the picture.

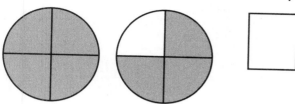

b) Write a mixed number for the picture.

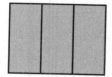  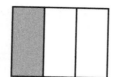

7. Circle the larger fraction.

a) $\frac{3}{8}$ or $\frac{5}{8}$ 　　　　b) $\frac{1}{2}$ or $\frac{1}{3}$ 　　　　c) $\frac{2}{5}$ or $\frac{2}{3}$

8. Ava, Sun, Ravi, and Will share a pizza. Ava and Sun each take $\frac{1}{3}$ of the pizza. Ravi and Will split the last piece.

a) What fraction of the pizza did Ava and Sun eat altogether?

b) What fraction of the pizza is left for Ravi and Will?

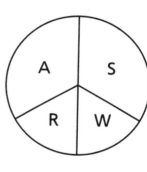

c) What fraction did Ravi and Will each get?

9. What fraction of the whole square is each labeled part?

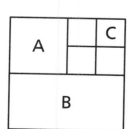

A = ☐ 　　　　B = ☐ 　　　　**BONUS ▶ C =** ☐

1. Write the number of balls on each table. Write = if the tables have the same number. Write ≠ if they do not have the same number.

a)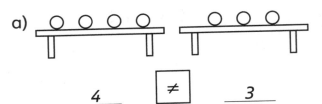

<u> 4 </u> $\boxed{\neq}$ <u> 3 </u>

b)

<u>   </u> $\boxed{}$ <u>   </u>

c)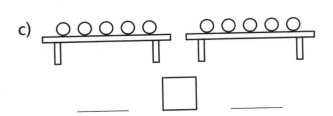

<u>   </u> $\boxed{}$ <u>   </u>

d)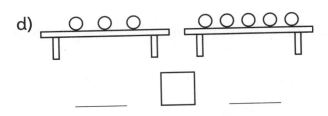

<u>   </u> $\boxed{}$ <u>   </u>

2. Write the number of balls. Write = or ≠ in the box.

a)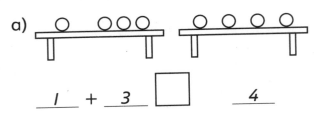

<u> 1 </u> + <u> 3 </u> $\boxed{}$ <u> 4 </u>

b)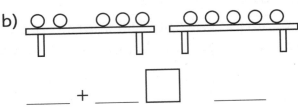

<u>   </u> + <u>   </u> $\boxed{}$ <u>   </u>

c)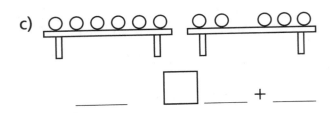

<u>   </u> $\boxed{}$ <u>   </u> + <u>   </u>

d)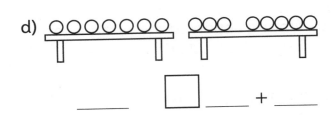

<u>   </u> $\boxed{}$ <u>   </u> + <u>   </u>

e)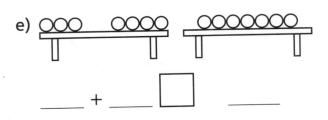

<u>   </u> + <u>   </u> $\boxed{}$ <u>   </u>

f)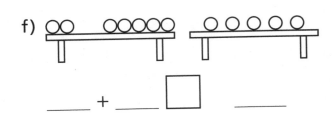

<u>   </u> + <u>   </u> $\boxed{}$ <u>   </u>

g)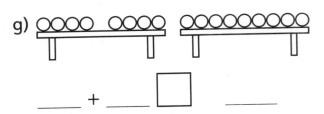

<u>   </u> + <u>   </u> $\boxed{}$ <u>   </u>

h)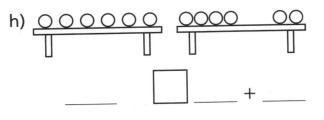

<u>   </u> $\boxed{}$ <u>   </u> + <u>   </u>

3. Circle the correct addition sentence.

a) $\boxed{7 = 3 + 4}$ b) $9 = 5 + 3$ c) $8 = 6 + 2$

   $7 \neq 3 + 4$ $\boxed{9 \neq 5 + 3}$ $8 \neq 6 + 2$

d) $5 = 3 + 1$ e) $11 + 5 = 16$ f) $12 + 3 = 15$

   $5 \neq 3 + 1$ $11 + 5 \neq 16$ $12 + 3 \neq 15$

An **equation** is a number sentence that has an **equal sign** (=).

$$3 + 5 = 8$$

equal sign

The equal sign shows that the left side of the number sentence has the same value as the right side.

---

4. Circle the number sentences that are equations.

A. $5 + 7 \neq 13$ **B.** $6 < 9$ **C.** $15 - 2 = 13$

D. $4 = 32 \div 8$ **E.** $6 \times 5 > 15$ **F.** $14 \neq 12 + 3$

5. Write "T" if the equation is true. Write "F" if the equation is false.

a) $3 + 7 = 10$ ___T___   b) $9 + 4 = 12$ ___F___   c) $2 + 17 = 18$ _____

d) $6 - 2 = 4$ _____   e) $24 - 5 = 19$ _____   f) $25 - 13 = 11$ _____

g) $3 \times 9 = 27$ _____   h) $6 \times 7 = 42$ _____   i) $56 = 8 \times 8$ _____

j) $24 \div 4 = 8$ _____   k) $12 \div 3 = 4$ _____   l) $6 = 35 \div 5$ _____

m) $14 + 13 = 27$ _____   n) $9 \times 3 = 28$ _____   o) $9 = 45 \div 5$ _____

p) $18 - 12 = 7$ _____   q) $4 = 15 - 10$ _____   r) $8 = 80 \div 10$ _____

BONUS ▶

s) $2 + 4 = 3 \times 2$ _____   t) $5 + 6 = 14 - 2$ _____   u) $24 \div 6 = 10 - 6$ _____

OA3-57 Unknown Numbers in Equations (I)

1. Some apples are inside a box and some are outside. Draw the missing apples in the box.

a)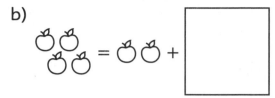

total number
of apples

b)

c)

d)

2. Draw the missing apples in the box. Then write the missing number in the smaller box.

a)

5 = 3 + 2

b)

8 = 3 + ☐

c)

3 + ☐ = 4

d)

4 + ☐ = 7

Finding the missing number in an equation is called **solving** the equation.

3. Draw a picture for the equation. Use your picture to solve the equation.

a) 5 + ☐ = 6

b) ☐ + 4 = 9

OA3-58 Using Letters for Unknown Numbers

1. Solve the equation by guessing and checking.

a) $\boxed{} + 3 = 4$

b) $\boxed{} + 3 = 5$

c) $\boxed{} + 5 = 7$

d) $2 + \boxed{} = 6$

e) $2 + \boxed{} = 7$

f) $8 = \boxed{} + 5$

2. Sam took some apples from a box. Write how many apples were in the box before.

a)

Sam took away this many.　This many were left.

b)

c)

d)

3. Solve the equation by guessing and checking.

a) $\boxed{} - 2 = 2$

b) $\boxed{} - 4 = 3$

c) $\boxed{} - 3 = 3$

d) $5 - \boxed{} = 1$

e) $7 - \boxed{} = 2$

f) $6 - \boxed{} = 4$

You can use a letter to stand for the number you do not know.

$\boxed{} + 5 = 8$ can be written as $x + 5 = 8$ or $b + 5 = 8$.

---

4. Solve the equation.

a) $x + 3 = 5$

b) $x + 7 = 10$

c) $x - 2 = 5$

$x = \underline{}$

$x = \underline{}$

$x = \underline{}$

d) $10 - a = 6$

e) $4 + y = 9$

f) $11 = m + 3$

$a = \underline{}$

$y = \underline{}$

$m = \underline{}$

OA3-59 Unknown Numbers in Equations (2)

1. Draw the same number of apples in each box. Write the equation for the picture.

a)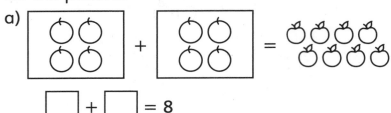

☐ + ☐ = 8

b)

☐ + ☐ + ☐ = 9

c)

☐ + ☐ + ☐ = 15

REMINDER ▶

Multiplication is a short form for repeated addition.

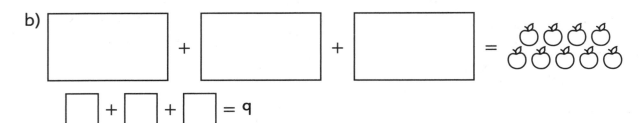

$\boxed{2}$ + $\boxed{2}$ + $\boxed{2}$ is the same as 3 × $\boxed{2}$

🍎🍎 + 🍎🍎 + 🍎🍎 is the same as 3 × 🍎🍎

2. Draw the missing apples in the box. Then write the missing number in the smaller box.

a)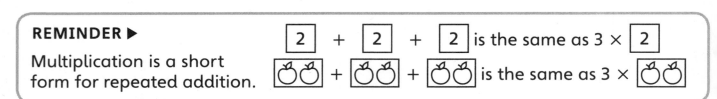

3 × $\boxed{2}$ = 6

b)

2 × ☐ = 8

c)

3 × ☐ = 15

d)

6 × ☐ = 18

3. How many apples should be in the box? Write the number.

a) $2 \times \boxed{3} = $ 🍎🍎🍎 🍎🍎🍎

b) $2 \times \boxed{} = $ 🍎🍎 🍎🍎

c) $\boxed{} \times 3 = $ 🍎🍎🍎 🍎🍎🍎

d) $\boxed{} \times 4 = $ 🍎🍎🍎🍎 🍎🍎🍎🍎

e) $\boxed{} \times 5 = $ 🍎🍎🍎🍎🍎 🍎🍎🍎🍎🍎

f) $\boxed{} \times 2 = $ 🍎🍎🍎🍎 🍎🍎🍎🍎

g) $3 \times$ 🍎🍎🍎 🍎🍎🍎 $= \boxed{}$

h) $8 \times$ 🍎🍎 🍎🍎 $= \boxed{}$

4. Solve the equation.

a) $5 \times \boxed{} = 10$

b) $4 \times \boxed{} = 12$

c) $\boxed{} \times 3 = 21$

d) $8 \times \boxed{} = 64$

e) $\boxed{} \times 9 = 27$

f) $14 = \boxed{} \times 2$

g) $\boxed{} \div 3 = 2$

h) $\boxed{} \div 4 = 4$

i) $\boxed{} \div 5 = 7$

j) $\boxed{} \div 6 = 7$

k) $\boxed{} \div 8 = 6$

l) $28 = \boxed{} \times 7$

5. Solve the equation.

a) $3 \times a = 18$

b) $4 \times b = 20$

c) $b \times 3 = 21$

$a = \underline{}$

$b = \underline{}$

$b = \underline{}$

d) $y \times 6 = 42$

e) $5 \times t = 25$

BONUS ▶ $a + a = 12$

$y = \underline{}$

$t = \underline{}$

$a = \underline{}$

> You can write a story for an addition equation.
>
> Example: $\boxed{} + 2 = 5$
>
> Story: Peter had some stickers.
> His friend gave him 2 more stickers.
> Now Peter has 5 stickers in total.

1. Write a story for the equation.

   a) $\boxed{} + 2 = 7$

   _____

   _____

   b) $\boxed{} + 4 = 8$

   _____

   _____

> You can write a story for a multiplication equation.
>
> Example: $3 \times \boxed{} = 12$
>
> Story: There are 3 boxes.
> Each box has the same number of apples.
> There are 12 apples altogether.

2. Write a story for the equation.

   a) $4 \times \boxed{} = 8$

   b) $2 \times \boxed{} = 6$

   c) $5 \times \boxed{} = 35$

   BONUS ▶ $\boxed{} - 2 = 6$

BONUS ▶ Write an equation for the story. Solve the equation.

   a) Kim had some apples.
      She bought 3 more apples.
      Now she has 8 apples altogether.

   b) There are 4 boxes.
      Each box has the same
      number of oranges.
      There are 8 oranges altogether.

OA3-61 Tape Diagrams (I)

Jane draws a **tape diagram** to compare the numbers 10 and 6.

She draws 2 **bars** and labels them.   She adds 10 + 6 to find the total.

She subtracts 10 − 6 to find the difference.

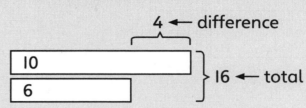

1. Fill in the total or the missing number.

a)
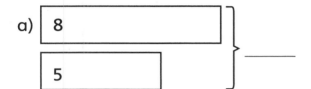

b)

9

4

c)
7

10

d)

3
9

e)
10
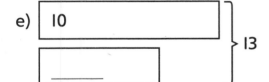
13

f)
17
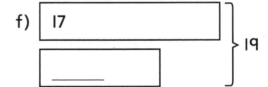
19

g)
25

67

h)
42
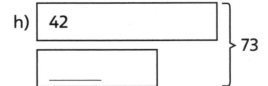
73

BONUS ▶

i)
314
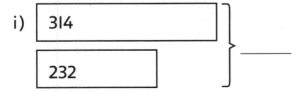
232

j)
401
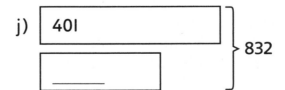
832

2. Fill in the difference or the missing number.

a)
8
5

b)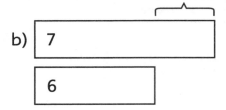
7
6

c)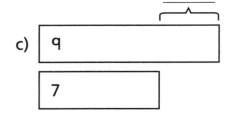
9
7

d)
6
4

e)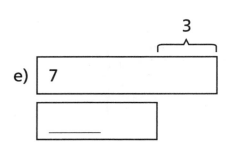
3
7
_____

f)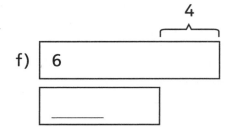
4
6
_____

3. Find the missing number.

a)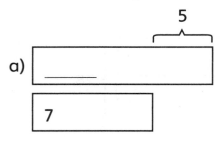
5
_____
7

b)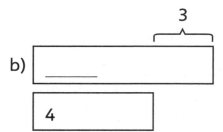
3
_____
4

c)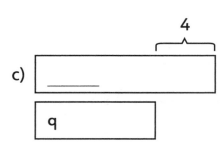
4
_____
9

d)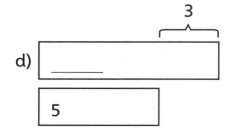
3
_____
5

4. Fill in the blanks.

a)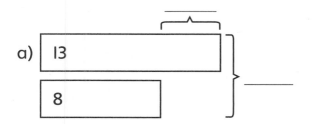

b)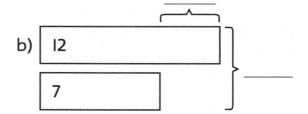

c)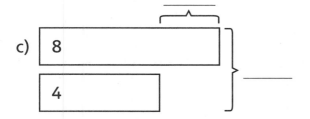

d)

e)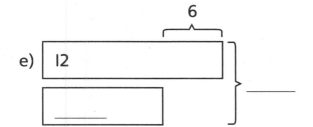

f)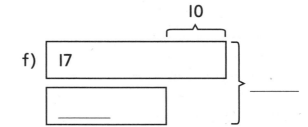

g)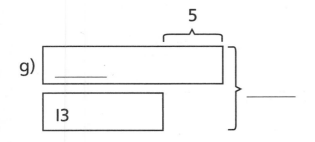

h)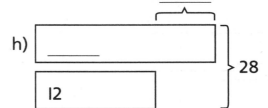

BONUS ▶

i)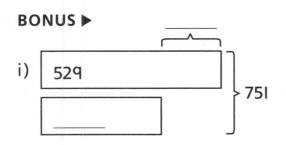

j)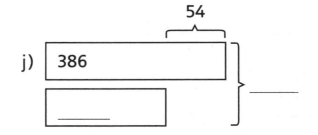

I. Underline the part that is larger. Write the name of that part beside the longer bar. Fill in the blanks.

a) 8 <u>apples</u> and 5 oranges

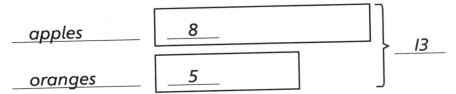

<u>apples</u> | 8 |
<u>oranges</u> | 5 | } 13

b) 4 red fish and 9 blue fish

c) 13 pens and 12 pencils

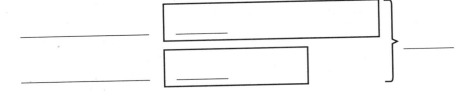

d) 11 plates and 16 cups

BONUS ▶ 9 apples in total
5 are red and the rest are green

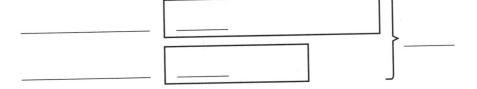

2. Underline the part that is larger. Write the name of that part beside the longer bar. Fill in the blanks.

a) 3 more cats than dogs
   5 dogs

b) 10 more spoons than forks
   4 forks

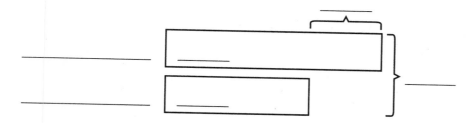

c) 4 fewer girls than boys
   12 boys

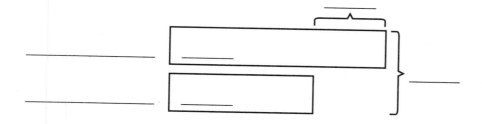

d) 6 fewer science books than art books
   8 science books

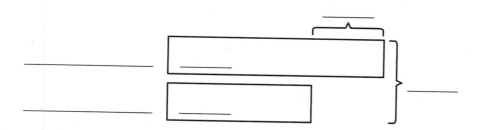

3. Fill in the blanks.

a) 9 lions and 7 tigers

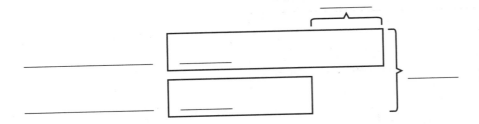

b) 9 more girls than boys
   13 girls

c) 6 more boys than girls
   5 girls

BONUS ▶ Karen has 12 apples in total.
8 are green. The others are red.

Operations and Algebraic Thinking 3-62

4. There are 24 students in a class. 14 are boys.

    a) Fill in the blanks.

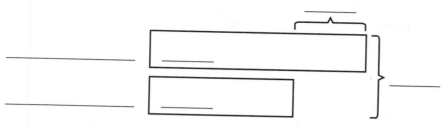

    b) How many girls are in the class? _____

    c) How many more boys than girls are there? _____

5. Alan has 5 more US stamps than Canadian stamps.
He has 12 Canadian stamps.

    a) Fill in the blanks.

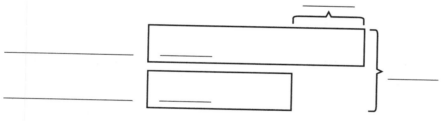

    b) How many stamps does he have in total? _____

6. Sally rode her bike 252 miles to raise money for charity.
Kevin rode his bike 57 miles.

    a) Draw a tape diagram to show this information.

    b) How much farther did Sally ride?

    c) How many miles did they ride altogether?

BONUS ▶ Hint: Use a tape diagram with 3 bars.

    a) A store sold 8 books on Friday.
       They sold 5 fewer books on Thursday than on Friday.
       They sold 4 more books on Saturday than on Friday.
       How many books did the store sell on the three days?

    b) Ivan has 12 green apples.
       He has 7 more red apples than green apples.
       He has 3 fewer yellow apples than red apples.
       How many apples does he have altogether?

Books for sale

OA3-63 Rows and Columns

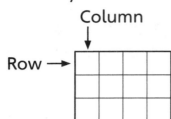

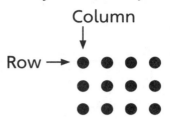

1. Number the rows and columns. Write the total number of small squares in the array.

a)
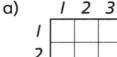

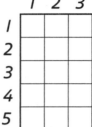

___5___ rows

___3___ columns

total ___5 × 3 = 15___

or ___3 × 5 = 15___

b)
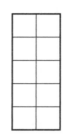

_____ rows

_____ columns

total _____

or _____

c)
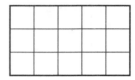

_____ rows

_____ columns

total _____

or _____

2. Count the rows and columns. Write the total number of dots in the array.

a)

___4___ rows

___3___ columns

total ___4 × 3 = 12___

or ___3 × 4 = 12___

b)

_____ rows

_____ columns

total _____

or _____

c)
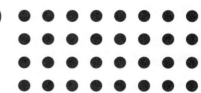

_____ rows

_____ columns

total _____

or _____

3. Write a multiplication equation for the total number of dots.
Then write another multiplication equation and two division
equations for the array.

a)

● ● ● ● ●
● ● ● ● ●
● ● ● ● ●

_3_ rows _5_ columns

total _3 × 5 = 15_

_5 × 3 = 15_

_15 ÷ 5 = 3_

_15 ÷ 3 = 5_

b)

● ● ● ● ● ●
● ● ● ● ● ●

_____ rows _____ columns

total _____

_____

_____

_____

4. The table gives the number of rows and columns for arrays.
Write two multiplication equations and two division equations
for each array.

	Rows	Columns	Total	Equations	
a)	5	2	10	5 × 2 = 10 2 × 5 = 10	10 ÷ 5 = 2 10 ÷ 2 = 5
b)	6	4	24		
c)	3	7	21		
d)	7	8	56		
e)	8	6	48		
f)	10	9	90		

5. The question mark (?) is the number we do not know. Write an equation that gives the unknown.

	Rows	Columns	Total	Equation
a)	3	5	?	$? = 3 \times 5$
b)	?	6	18	$? = 18 \div 6$
c)	?	2	16	
d)	4	?	36	
e)	7	8	?	
f)	9	?	45	

6. Ken plants 8 rows of trees. He plants 3 trees in each row. How many trees does he plant? Draw an array of dots to show your answer.

7. Randi arranges 35 chairs in rows with 5 chairs in each row. How many rows of chairs did she make?

8. Beth plants 12 flowers in 3 rows. How many flowers are in each row?

9. Mona arranges 9 rows of beads with 7 beads in each row. How many beads are in her array?

BONUS ▶ John makes an array using dimes. He makes 2 rows with 4 dimes in each row.

  a) How many dimes did John use?

  b) How much money did John use?

BONUS ▶ Marco plants 6 rows of trees with 4 in each row. Tom plants 7 rows of trees with 3 in each row. How many more trees did Marco plant?

BONUS ▶ Wendy arranges 36 stickers with 6 in each row. Raj arranges 49 stickers with 7 in each row. Who made more rows?

Operations and Algebraic Thinking 3-63

OA3-64 Problems with Multiplication and Division

1. Write two multiplication equations and two division equations for the picture.

a)

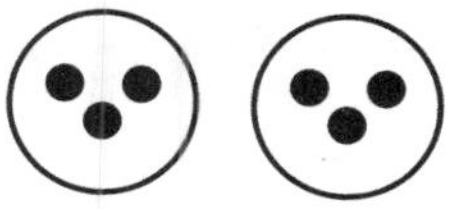

2 groups

3 in each group

6 in total

$2 \times 3 = 6$

$3 \times 2 = 6$

$6 \div 2 = 3$

$6 \div 3 = 2$

b)

_____ groups

_____ in each group

_____ in total

____

____

____

____

c)

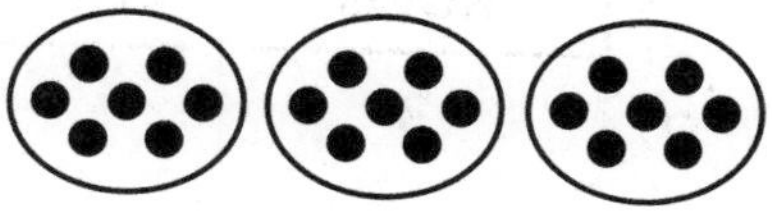

_____ groups

_____ in each group

_____ in total

____

____

____

____

2. Write two multiplication equations and two division equations for each row in the table.

	Number of Groups	Number in Each Group	Total	Equations
a)	3	7	21	$3 \times 7 = 21$ $\quad 21 \div 3 = 7$ $7 \times 3 = 21$ $\quad 21 \div 7 = 3$
b)	9	5	45	
c)	7	6	42	
d)	8	4	32	

3. Write a question mark (?) for the amount you do not know.
Then write an equation that solves the problem.

Problem	Number of Groups	Number in Each Group	Total	Equation
a) 3 pears in each basket 12 pears How many baskets?	?	3	12	? = 12 ÷ 3
b) 4 toys in each box 6 boxes How many toys?				
c) 5 birds on each branch 35 birds How many branches?				
d) 3 children in each boat 12 children in total How many boats?				
e) 3 tents 15 children How many children in each tent?				
f) 5 rows of trees 40 trees How many in each row?				
g) 30 bananas 6 bananas in each bag How many bags?				
h) 9 pennies in each pocket 4 pockets How many pennies in total?				

4. There are 2 hamsters in each classroom. How many hamsters are in 8 classrooms?

5. Clara bought 24 stamps. There are 8 stamps in each pack. How many packs did she buy?

6. Anwar put 32 granola bars in 8 boxes. He put the same number in each box. How many did he put in each box?

7. Zack bought 8 packs of pens with 5 pens in each pack. Yu bought 9 packs of pens with 4 pens in each pack.

a) How many pens did Zack buy?

b) How many pens did Yu buy?

c) Who bought more pens?

8. Alex planted 24 flowers with 3 in each row. Marco planted 42 flowers with 6 in each row. Who planted more rows?

9. Rani planted 18 trees in 3 rows. Nina planted 24 trees in 6 rows. How many more trees are in Rani's rows than in Nina's rows?

10. A chess team has 4 players. School A sent 20 players to a chess match. School B sent 32 players to the match. How many more teams did School B send?

11. A basketball team has 5 players. School A sent 7 teams to a basketball match. School B sent 8 teams to the match. How many players did School A and School B send altogether?

BONUS ▶ A rubber raft costs $8 and can hold 3 children. There are 12 children who want to buy rafts.

a) How many rafts should the children buy?

b) How much will all the rafts cost?

OA3-65 Multistep Problems

1. Mark has 28 pears. He eats 4 and gives the rest to 3 friends.
Each friend gets the same number of pears.

   a) How many pears are left after Mark eats 4 of them?

   b) How many pears does each of Mark's friends get?

2. Anna has 12 books. Then she buys 6 more and puts all the books
in 3 boxes. She puts the same number of books in each box.

   a) How many books does Anna have in total?

   b) How many books does she put in each box?

3. 32 children go camping. They put up 6 tents.
Each tent holds 4 children.

   a) How many tents do 32 children need?

   b) How many more tents do they need to put up?

4. Mary has 23 fossils and Ben has 25 fossils.
They put all their fossils in a display case.
If they put 8 fossils on each shelf, how many shelves do they use?

5. 6 students want to buy pizzas for a school party. Each student
has $5. A pizza costs $10. How many pizzas can they buy?

6. Lucy earns $10 each week shoveling snow.
She spends $4 each week and saves the rest of her money.
How much money will she save in 3 weeks?

7. Amy earns $15 each week doing chores.
She spends $7 each week and saves the rest of her money.
How much money will she save in 9 weeks?

BONUS ▶ 4 children pick 20 apples and share them equally.
Each child eats 2 apples.

   a) How many apples does each child have after they
eat the apples?

   b) How many apples do they now have in total?

8. Anna has 9 five-dollar bills. Ravi has 7 ten-dollar bills.

   a) How much money does Anna have?

   b) How much money does Ravi have?

   c) How much money do they have altogether?

9. Kate has 4 five-dollar bills. She wants to buy 7 light bulbs. Each light bulb costs $3.

   a) How much money does Kate have?

   b) How much do 7 light bulbs cost?

   c) Does she have enough money to buy the bulbs?

10. Tim bought 30 stamps in packs of 6. Josh bought 32 stamps in packs of 8. Who bought more packs of stamps?

11. Ben ran 10 blocks on Saturday and 7 blocks on Sunday. Zara ran 8 blocks on Saturday and 11 blocks on Sunday. Who ran more, Ben or Zara?

12. Jon plants 3 rows of flowers with 7 in each row. Alexa plants 8 rows of flowers with 5 in each row. How many flowers do they plant altogether?

13. Ellen buys 9 crayons that cost 8¢ each. Ava buys 7 erasers that cost 10¢ each. How much more money does Ellen spend than Ava?

14. Zack buys 10 pencils that cost 6 cents each. Ali buys 4 pens that cost 9 cents each. How much money do Zack and Ali spend altogether?

BONUS ▶ Ed slices 18 mushrooms to add to 3 pizzas. Ross uses 24 mushrooms for 6 pizzas.

   a) Who uses more mushrooms for 1 pizza?

   b) If Ross and Ed each make 1 pizza, how many mushrooms will they need?

OA3-66 More Multistep Problems (Advanced)

When you solve a word problem, you can use brackets to show what happens first.

A teacher has 21 stickers. She buys 4 more. Then 5 of her students share them equally.

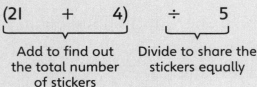

$$(21 + 4) \div 5$$

Add to find out the total number of stickers

Divide to share the stickers equally

I. Use brackets to show what happens first.

a) A teacher has 25 stickers.
   She buys 5 more.
   Then she shares them equally among 6 students.

   $(25 + 5) \div 6$

b) A teacher has 19 books.
   He buys 8 more.
   Then he shares them equally among 9 students.

   _____

c) There are 9 pumpkins in a garden.
   3 more grow.
   4 children share them equally.

   _____

d) Kyle has 14 plums.
   He eats 2.
   Then he gives the rest to 3 friends to share equally.

   _____

e) Sarah has 19 bananas.
   She eats 1.
   6 monkeys share the rest equally.

   _____

f) Ali has 3 muffins.
   He bakes 12 more.
   5 friends share the muffins equally.

   _____

BONUS ▶

g) 9 children have 20 pencils.
   They use 2 of them.
   They share the pencils that are left equally.

   _____

h) 8 children have 12 apples.
   They pick 4 more.
   Then they share them equally.

   _____

Use brackets to show which operation is done first.

Paul has 7 boxes.
There are 3 pens in each box.
He puts 2 more pens in each box.
How many pens are in the boxes now?

Number of pens = $(3 + 2) \times 7$

2. Write an equation for the problem. Use x for the number you are trying to find.

a) A farmer has 3 barns.
There are 6 cows in each barn.
The farmer lets 2 more cows into each barn.
How many cows are in the barns now?

$x =$ _$(6 + 2) \times 3$_

b) Helen has 4 brothers.
Each brother has 3 stickers.
She gives each brother 5 more stickers.
How many stickers do the brothers have now?

$x =$ _____

c) Sara buys 6 books for $4 each.
She buys a book bag for $10.
How much did she spend?

$x =$ _____

d) Bev buys 5 tennis balls for $3 each.
Then she buys a tennis racket for $50.
How much did she spend?

$x =$ _____

3. Write an equation and find the answer.

a) Jen keeps 5 fish in each of 5 aquariums.
She adds 2 more fish to each aquarium.
How many fish does she have now?

$x =$ _$(5 + 2) \times 5$_

$x =$ _7×5_

$x =$ _35_

b) There are 6 gardens.
Each garden has 3 flowers.
5 more flowers grow in each garden.
How many flowers are there now?

$x =$ _____

$x =$ _____

$x =$ _____

NBT3-16 Multiplying Tens

To multiply 4 × 30, Tina makes 4 groups of 3 tens blocks (30 = 3 tens).

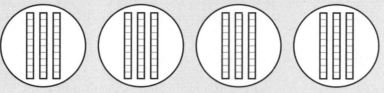

4 × 30 = 4 × 3 tens = 12 tens = 120

Tina notices a pattern: 4 × 3 = 12   **4 × 30 = 120**

1. Draw a picture to show the multiplication. Then find the answer.

a) 3 × 20

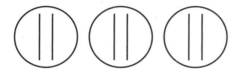

3 × 20 = 3 × __2__ tens = __6__ tens = __60__

b) 2 × 40

2 × 40 = 2 × ______ tens = ______ tens = ______

c) 2 × 30

2 × 30 = 2 × ______ tens = ______ tens = ______

d) 5 × 20

5 × 20 = 5 × ______ tens = ______ tens = ______

e) 3 × 30

3 × 30 = 3 × ______ tens = ______ tens = ______

2. Multiply by using tens.

    a) $3 \times 60 = 3 \times$ __6__ tens $=$ __18__ tens $=$ __180__

    b) $7 \times 70 = 7 \times$ _____ tens $=$ _____ tens $=$ _____

    c) $6 \times 70 = 6 \times$ _____ tens $=$ _____ tens $=$ _____

    d) $8 \times 60 = 8 \times$ _____ tens $=$ _____ tens $=$ _____

    e) $4 \times 90 = 4 \times$ _____ tens $=$ _____ tens $=$ _____

3. Multiply.

    a) $2 \times 3 =$ __6__
          b) $4 \times 2 =$ _____
          c) $3 \times 3 =$ _____

       $2 \times 30 =$ __60__
             $4 \times 20 =$ _____
             $3 \times 30 =$ _____

    d) $7 \times 4 =$ _____
          e) $4 \times 4 =$ _____
          f) $2 \times 8 =$ _____

       $7 \times 40 =$ _____
             $4 \times 40 =$ _____
             $2 \times 80 =$ _____

    g) $5 \times 2 =$ _____
          h) $6 \times 3 =$ _____
          i) $5 \times 7 =$ _____

       $5 \times 20 =$ _____
             $6 \times 30 =$ _____
             $5 \times 70 =$ _____

4. Multiply.

    a) $7 \times 30 =$ __210__
          b) $2 \times 60 =$ _____
          c) $8 \times 30 =$ _____

    d) $5 \times 70 =$ _____
          e) $4 \times 90 =$ _____
          f) $60 \times 7 =$ _____

    g) $8 \times 80 =$ _____
          h) $90 \times 6 =$ _____
          i) $80 \times 9 =$ _____

5. You know that $2 \times 4 = 8$. How can you use this fact to multiply 2×40?

6. Museum A has 4 boxes with 60 seashells in each box. Museum B has 8 boxes with 40 seashells in each box. Which museum has more shells?

NBT3-17 Rounding (Tens)

> Multiples of 10 are the numbers you say when counting by tens starting at 0.
> 0, 10, 20, 30, 40, 50, 60, 70, 80, 90, 100, and so on.

1. Find the multiple of 10 that comes after the number.

   a) 23, __30__   b) 64, _____   c) 78, _____   **BONUS ▶** 101, _____

2. Find the multiple of 10 that comes before the number.

   a) __40__, 46   b) _____, 85   c) _____, 22   **BONUS ▶** _____, 109

3. Find the multiples of 10 before and after the number.

   a) __40__, 43, __50__   b) _____, 67, _____   c) _____, 18, _____

   d) _____, 71, _____   e) _____, 7, _____   f) _____, 35, _____

4. Draw an arrow to show if the circled number is closer to the
   multiple of 10 that comes before or after the number.

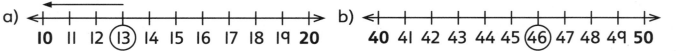

a) 10 11 12 (13) 14 15 16 17 18 19 20   b) 40 41 42 43 44 45 (46) 47 48 49 50

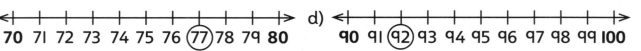

c) 70 71 72 73 74 75 76 (77) 78 79 80   d) 90 91 (92) 93 94 95 96 97 98 99 100

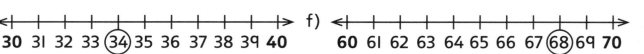

e) 30 31 32 33 (34) 35 36 37 38 39 40   f) 60 61 62 63 64 65 66 67 (68) 69 70

5. Look at your answers to Question 4.

   a) List the ones digits of the numbers that are closer to the **previous**

      multiple of 10. _____

   b) List the ones digits of the numbers that are closer to the **next**

      multiple of 10. _____

   c) Why are the numbers with a ones digit of 5 a special case?

   _____

When **rounding** to the nearest multiple of 10:

If the ones digit is 1, 2, 3, or 4, **round down** to the previous multiple of 10.

If the ones digit is 5, 6, 7, 8, or 9, **round up** to the next multiple of 10.

Examples: 53 rounds down to 50.   47 rounds up to 50.

6. Round to the nearest multiple of 10. Circle the answer.

a) 58 is rounded to   50   or   (60)   b) 32 is rounded to   30   or   40

c) 64 is rounded to   60   or   70   d) 21 is rounded to   20   or   30

e) 77 is rounded to   70   or   80   f) 25 is rounded to   20   or   30

7. Draw an arrow to show if the circled number is closer to the previous or next multiple of 10.

a)
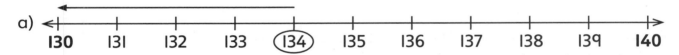

b)
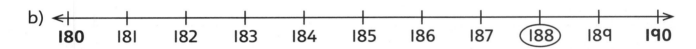

c)
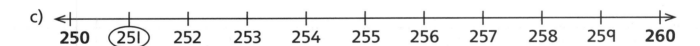

d)
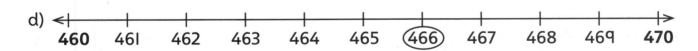

8. Find the previous and next multiple of 10.

a) _140_ , 143, _150_   b) _____, 123, _____   c) _____, 158, _____

d) _____, 262, _____   e) _____, 381, _____   f) _____, 409, _____

g) _____, 514, _____   h) _____, 635, _____   i) _____, 777, _____

BONUS ▶

j) _____, 892, _____   k) _____, 999, _____

9. Round to the nearest ten. Circle the answer.

a) 138 is rounded to   130   or   (140)

b) 123 is rounded to   120   or   130

c) 267 is rounded to   260   or   270

d) 241 is rounded to   240   or   250

e) 459 is rounded to   450   or   460

f) 706 is rounded to   700   or   710

g) 692 is rounded to   690   or   700

h) 965 is rounded to   960   or   970

10. Find the previous and the next multiple of 10. Which would you round the number to? Circle it.

a) 27   _20_   or   (30)

b) 43   _____   or   _____

c) 89   _____   or   _____

d) 65   _____   or   _____

e) 126   _____   or   _____

f) 239   _____   or   _____

g) 213   _____   or   _____

h) 368   _____   or   _____

i) 832   _____   or   _____

j) 949   _____   or   _____

11. Round to the nearest ten.

a) 62   [60]

b) 86   [   ]

c) 136   [   ]

d) 261   [   ]

e) 476   [   ]

f) 307   [   ]

g) 819   [   ]

h) 989   [   ]

i) 745   [   ]

j) 558   [   ]

12. Sam has 287 baseball cards. Rounded to the nearest ten, how many baseball cards does he have?

NBT3-18 Rounding (Hundreds)

> You can find the multiples of 100 by counting by hundreds starting at 0:
>
> 0, 100, 200, 300, 400, 500, 600, and so on.

1. Find the multiple of 100 that comes after the number.

   a) 365, __400__   b) 817, _____   c) 605, _____

   d) 739, _____   e) 241, _____   f) 752, _____

2. Find the multiple of 100 that comes before the number.

   a) __200__, 261   b) _____, 452   c) _____, 550

   d) _____, 128   e) _____, 637   f) _____, 794

3. Find the previous and next multiple of 100.

   a) __300__, 362, __400__   b) _____, 475, _____   c) _____, 732, _____

   d) _____, 819, _____   e) _____, 206, _____   f) _____, 317, _____

4. Draw an arrow to show whether the circled number is closer to the
   previous or next multiple of 100.

   a)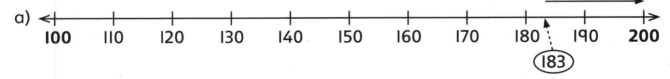

   b)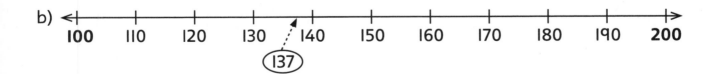

   c)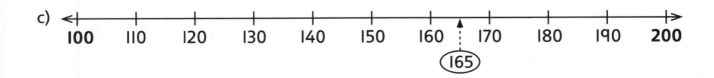

5. Draw an arrow to show whether the circled number is closer to the previous or the next multiple of 100.

a)
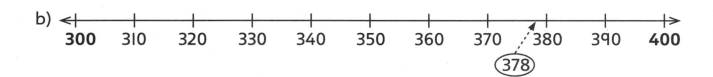

b)
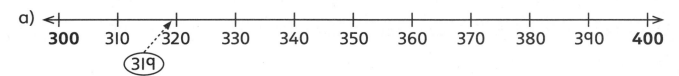

c)
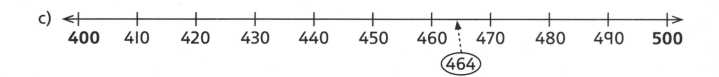

d)
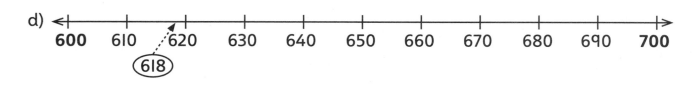

The numbers less than 150 are closer to 100 than to 200.

The numbers greater than 150 are closer to 200 than to 100.

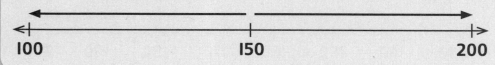

6. Circle the answer.

a) 153 is closer to   100   or   (200)   b) 729 is closer to   700   or   800

c) 319 is closer to   300   or   400   d) 542 is closer to   500   or   600

e) 586 is closer to   500   or   600   f) 682 is closer to   600   or   700

g) 207 is closer to   200   or   300   h) 418 is closer to   400   or   500

7. Explain why 150 is a special case.

When rounding to the nearest multiple of 100:

If the tens digit is 0, 1, 2, 3, or 4, round down to the previous multiple of 100.

If the tens digit is 5, 6, 7, 8, or 9, round up to the next multiple of 100.

Examples: 632 rounds to 600.   258 rounds to 300.

8. Round to the nearest hundred. Circle the answer.

a) 257 is rounded to   200   or   (300)   b) 358 is rounded to   300   or   400

c) 275 is rounded to   200   or   300   d) 613 is rounded to   600   or   700

e) 850 is rounded to   800   or   900   f) 123 is rounded to   100   or   200

9. Find the previous and the next multiple of 100. Which would you round the number to? Circle it.

a) 386   _300_   or   (400)   b) 127   _____   or   _____

c) 802   _____   or   _____   d) 650   _____   or   _____

e) 932   _____   or   _____   f) 491   _____   or   _____

g) 321   _____   or   _____   h) 543   _____   or   _____

10. Round to the nearest hundred.

a) 831   _800_   b) 905   _____   c) 381   _____   d) 488   _____

e) 549   _____   f) 712   _____   g) 657   _____   h) 204   _____

11. Round the number two ways: to the nearest ten, and to the nearest hundred.

a) 315   b) 287   c) 861   d) 732

12. May has 270 stamps. Rounded to the nearest hundred, how many stamps does she have?

NBT3-19 Estimating

> **REMINDER** ▶ To round to the nearest ten, look at the ones digit.
> Round down if the ones digit is 1, 2, 3, or 4.
> Round up if the ones digit is 5, 6, 7, 8, or 9.
> Examples: 84 rounds to 80.   27 rounds to 30.

1. Round to the nearest ten.

a) 14 $\boxed{10}$ b) 23 $\boxed{}$ c) 72 $\boxed{}$

d) 145 $\boxed{150}$ e) 172 $\boxed{}$ f) 323 $\boxed{}$

g) 255 $\boxed{}$ h) 794 $\boxed{}$ i) 667 $\boxed{}$

j) 528 $\boxed{}$ k) 985 $\boxed{}$ l) 834 $\boxed{}$

> **REMINDER** ▶ To round to the nearest hundred, look at the tens digit.
> Round down if the tens digit is 1, 2, 3, or 4.
> Round up if the tens digit is 5, 6, 7, 8, or 9.

2. Round the number to the nearest hundred.

a) 340 $\boxed{300}$ b) 870 $\boxed{}$ c) 650 $\boxed{}$

d) 490 $\boxed{}$ e) 148 $\boxed{}$ f) 218 $\boxed{}$

g) 321 $\boxed{}$ h) 678 $\boxed{}$ i) 543 $\boxed{}$

3. Round to the nearest ten, then add or subtract.

a)   52 → $\boxed{50}$ b)   19 → $\boxed{}$ c)   47 → $\boxed{}$

+ 34 → + $\boxed{30}$ + 65 → +$\boxed{}$ − 11 → −$\boxed{}$

$\boxed{80}$

When you round numbers to the nearest ten or hundred, then calculate, you **estimate** the number.

4. Estimate by rounding each number to the nearest ten.

a) 32 + 28

$\underline{\quad 30 + 30 = 60 \quad}$

b) 74 − 33

c) 39 + 25

d) 82 − 57

e) 38 + 19

f) 52 + 49

g) 64 + 31

h) 75 + 22

i) 83 + 12

5. Estimate by rounding each number to the nearest hundred.

a)　　170　→　　200
　＋ 340　→　＋ 300
　　　　　　　　500

b)　　190　→
　＋ 650　→　＋

c)　　470　→
　− 110　→　−

d)　　640　→
　＋ 310　→

e)　　750　→
　＋ 220　→

f)　　830　→
　− 120　→

6. Estimate by rounding each number to the nearest hundred.

a) 540 + 210

b) 550 − 330

c) 210 + 770

d) 898 − 423

e) 390 − 211

f) 428 − 299

g) 856 − 198

h) 343 + 76

i) 576 + 285

7. Students collected donated coats. Round each number to the nearest ten, then add to estimate.

   a) Jon collected 34 coats and Beth collected 23 coats. How many coats did they collect altogether?

   b) Clara collected 86 coats and Mark collected 18 coats. How many coats did they collect altogether?

8. Students collected books to raise money for charity. Round each number to the nearest ten to estimate the difference between the numbers collected.

   a) Nina collected 58 books. David collected 43 books.

   b) Omar collected 84 books. Amy collected 72 books.

9. Three Grade 3 classes collected books. Round each number to the nearest hundred to answer.

Class	Number of Books
3A	258
3B	456
3C	645

   a) About how many books did class 3A and class 3B collect altogether?

   b) About how many more books did class 3C collect than class 3B?

   c) About how many books did all the Grade 3 classes (3A, 3B, and 3C) collect altogether?

NBT3-20 Place Value: Ones, Tens, Hundreds, and Thousands

> The place value to the left of the hundreds is the **thousands**.
>
>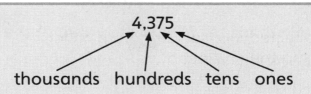
>
> 4,375
>
> thousands hundreds tens ones

I. Write the place value of the underlined digit.

a) 3,5<u>6</u>4   _tens_

b) 1,<u>3</u>36 _____

c) 25<u>6</u> _____

d) <u>1</u>,230 _____

e) <u>3</u>,859 _____

f) 5,<u>7</u>45 _____

2. Underline the digit 3, then write its place value.

a) <u>3</u>,640   _thousands_

b) 347 _____

c) 431 _____

d) 2,413 _____

e) 1,237 _____

f) 3,645 _____

REMINDER ▶ You can also write numbers by using a place value chart.

Example: 4,375

Thousands	Hundreds	Tens	Ones
4	3	7	5

---

3. Write the number by using the place value chart.

		Thousands	Hundreds	Tens	Ones
a)	3,287	3	2	8	7
b)	9,021				
c)	485				
d)	36				
e)	3,221				
f)	5,602				

The number 2,836 is a **4-digit number**.

- The **digit** 2 stands for 2,000. The **value** of the digit 2 is 2,000.
- The digit 8 stands for 800. The value of the digit 8 is 800.
- The digit 3 stands for 30. The value of the digit 3 is 30.
- The digit 6 stands for 6. The value of the digit 6 is 6.

4. Write the value of each digit.

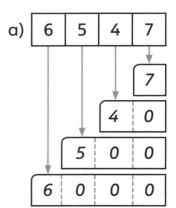

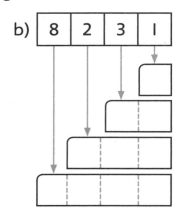

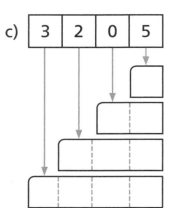

5. What does the digit 3 stand for in the number?

a) 632   [30]   b) 6,325 [   ]   c) 6,231 [   ]

d) 4,305 [   ]   e) 6,732 [   ]   f) 3,092 [   ]

g) 5,321 [   ]   h) 2,003 [   ]   i) 1,238 [   ]

6. Fill in the blanks.

a) In the number 6,572, the digit 5 stands for _____.

b) In the number 4,236, the digit 3 stands for _____.

c) In the number 8,021, the value of the digit 8 is _____.

d) In the number 2,387, the digit _____ is in the tens place.

e) In the number 3,729, the value of the digit 7 is _____.

f) In the number 9,845, the digit _____ is in the thousands place.

Adding to Make a 4-Digit Number

> Sometimes the sum of two 3-digit numbers is a 4-digit number.
>
> Example: 862 + 631
>
> | 8 hundreds + 6 tens + 2 ones | | 862 |
> |---|---|---|
> | 6 hundreds + 3 tens + 1 one | or | +   631 |
> | 14 hundreds + 9 tens + 3 ones | | 1,493 |
>
> after regrouping   1 thousand + 4 hundreds + 9 tens + 3 ones

1. Add the numbers.

a)

	3	8	5
+	9	1	1

b)

	4	2	3
+	6	1	4

c)

	8	6	0
+	5	3	0

d)

	2	1	7
+	9	7	0

e)

	3	8	2
+	8	1	6

f)

	1	1	5
+	8	2	1

g)

	6	3	6
+	4	4	0

h)

	9	1	2
+	9	1	7

i)

	6	2	5
+	8	0	2

2. Add. You might need to regroup once or twice.

a)

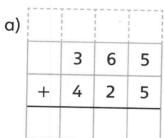

		3	6	5
	+	4	2	5

b)

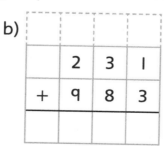

		2	3	1
	+	9	8	3

c)

		8	2	3
	+	5	4	7

3. Add. You might need to regroup three times.

a)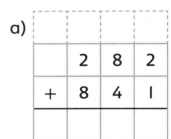

b)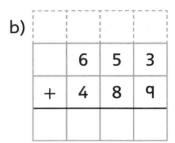

c)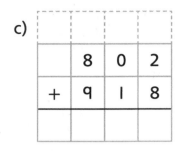

4. Write the numbers in the grid. Then add.

a) 282 + 510

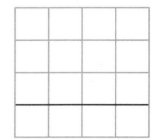

b) 627 + 932

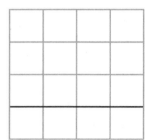

c) 512 + 739

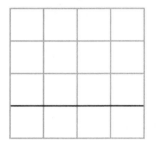

5. Estimate by rounding each number to the nearest hundred.
Then find the actual sum.

a) 327 + 452

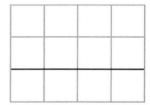 

Estimate   Sum

b) 823 + 456

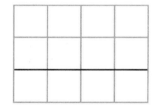 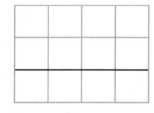

Estimate   Sum

6. Ross says the sum 231 + 118 + 397 will be greater than 1,000.
Is this reasonable? Explain.

BONUS ▶ Add or subtract.

a)   2,875
     + 3,121

b)   4,281
     + 3,814

c)   3,821
     −   210

d)   4,523
     − 3,109

e) 4,732 + 3,859

f) 4,891 − 2,193

1. Kevin says 372 + 215 is equal to 987. Estimate by rounding to the nearest hundred to check if his answer is reasonable.

   Estimate. _____

   Is his answer reasonable? _____

2. a) Circle the equations that are not correct.

244 + 382 = 526	357 − 283 = 174	586 + 394 = 970
354 + 372 = 726	983 − 438 = 545	875 − 538 = 136

   b) Explain how you found the answer.

3. Some friends collected cards. Add or subtract, and then estimate by rounding to the nearest ten to check if your answer is reasonable.

Name	Jayden	Robin	Henry	Kathy	Kayla
Number of Cards	432	346	228	315	227

   a) How many cards did Henry and Robin collect altogether?
   b) How many cards did Kathy and Kayla collect altogether?
   c) How many more cards did Jayden collect than Robin?
   d) How many more cards did Jayden collect than Kathy?

   BONUS ▶

   e) Which pair has more cards: Henry and Kayla or Robin and Kathy?

   f) What is the difference in part e)?

4. A store sells three kinds of fruit: apples, bananas, and oranges. One day, the store sold 300 pieces of fruit. If the store sold 152 apples and 75 bananas, how many oranges did it sell? First, estimate by rounding to the nearest ten. Then find the actual answer.

5. There are 38 students on one bus and 44 students on another.

   a) Estimate how many students are on the buses altogether.

   b) Find how many students are on the buses altogether.

   c) Each bus can hold 60 passengers. How many more students can fit on the two buses? How do you know?

6. Grace needs to travel 932 miles from Seattle, WA, to Carson City, NV. She travels 763 miles by train to Sacramento, CA, and then another 132 miles by train to Reno, NV. She takes a bus the rest of the way. How many miles does Grace travel by bus?

7. A museum display case can hold 100 insects. The display case has 27 dragonflies and 56 butterflies.

   a) Estimate how many more insects can be displayed.

   b) Check your estimate by adding and subtracting.

8. A tray of 4 plants costs 50¢. A tray of 6 plants costs 60¢.

   a) What is the cheapest way to buy 24 plants?

   b) What strategy did you use to solve the problem?

9. Estimate to answer the question. Then add or subtract to check.

   $57 $150 $62 $256

   a) How much do a bike and a hockey stick cost altogether?

   b) How much more does a canoe cost than a bike?

   c) Does all the equipment together cost more than $500?

Number and Operations in Base Ten 3-22

MD3-10 Digital Clocks

Digital clocks show both the hours and the minutes with two digits. The digital clock shows that 5 minutes have passed after 3 o'clock.

hours   minutes

We say the time is 3:05 or 5 minutes past 3.

1. Write the time in numbers.

a) **02:17**

_____2:17_____

b) **12:20**

_____

c) **01:03**

_____

2. Write the time in words and numbers.

a) **07:15**

___15 minutes past 7___

_____

b) **10:20**

_____

_____

c) **01:23**

_____

_____

d) **08:35**

_____

_____

e) **02:40**

_____

_____

f) **06:09**

_____

_____

3. Write the time the way it looks on a digital clock.

a) 7:01

| 0 | 7 | : | 0 | 1 |

b) 4:15

| | | : | | |

c) 3:08

| | | : | | |

d) 4 minutes past 9

| 0 | 9 | : | 0 | 4 |

e) 12 minutes past 12

| | | : | | |

f) 9 minutes past 11

| | | : | | |

g) 23 minutes past 2

| | | : | | |

h) 30 minutes past 6

| | | : | | |

i) 1 minute past 2

| | | : | | |

MD3-11 Analog Clock Faces and Hands

Analog clock faces show numbers from 1 to 12 in a circle.

To label a clock face, write in the numbers 12, 6, 3, and 9 first. Then fill in the rest of the numbers.

1. Fill in the missing numbers on the clock face.

a)

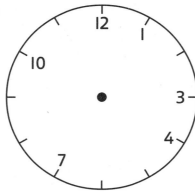

b)

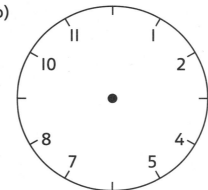

c)

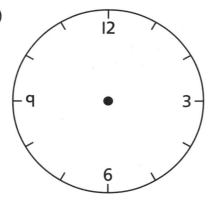

d)

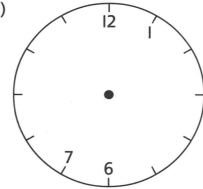

e)

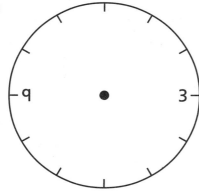

f)

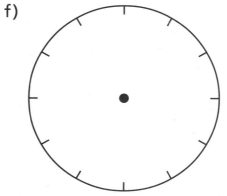

An analog clock face has different hands.

The **hour hand** is shorter.

The **minute hand** is longer.

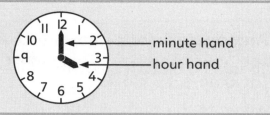

minute hand

hour hand

2. Which hand is shaded, the hour hand or the minute hand?

a)

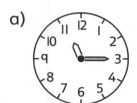

hour   (minute)

b)

hour   minute

c)

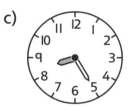

hour   minute

d)

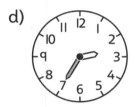

hour   minute

e)

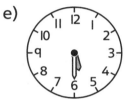

hour   minute

f)

hour   minute

g)

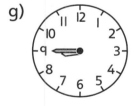

hour   minute

h)

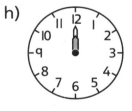

hour   minute

i)

hour   minute

j)

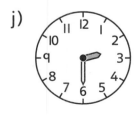

hour   minute

k)

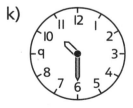

hour   minute

l)

hour   minute

3. How is an analog clock face the same as a number line? How is it different from a number line?

The minute hand points directly at 12.
The hour hand points directly at 3.
The time is 3 **o'clock**.

We write this time as 3:00.

1. Draw a line to show where the hour hand is pointing. Is it o'clock?
   Write "yes" or "no."

   a)

   _____

   b)

   _____

   c)

   _____

2. What time is it?

   a)

   __4__ : 00

   __4 o'clock__

   b)

   _____ : 00

   _____

   c)

   _____ : 00

   _____

   d)

   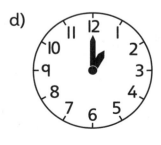

   _____ : 00

   _____

   e)

   _____ : 00

   _____

   f)

   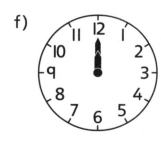

   _____ : 00

   _____

Both hands move from one number to the next.

When the hour hand points between the numbers 7 and 8, the hour is still 7.

3. Draw a line from the hour hand. Write the hour.

a)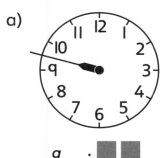

___q___ : ▮▮

b)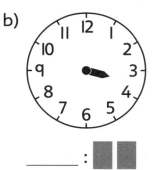

_____ : ▮▮

c)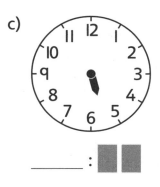

_____ : ▮▮

4. Circle the hour hand. Then write the hour.

a)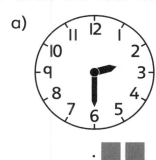

_____ : ▮▮

b)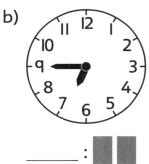

_____ : ▮▮

c)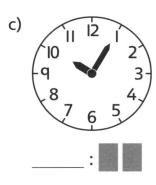

_____ : ▮▮

d)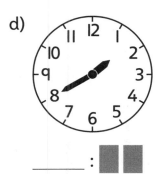

_____ : ▮▮

e)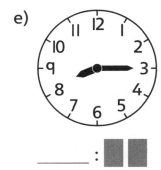

_____ : ▮▮

f)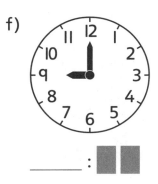

_____ : ▮▮

BONUS ▶ The numbers on the clock faces are missing! Match the clock to the time.

a) 5:00 _____

b) 9:00 _____

A.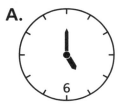

B.

When the minute hand moves from one number on the clock face to the next, 5 minutes have passed.

How many minutes is it past 9:00? Count by 5s.

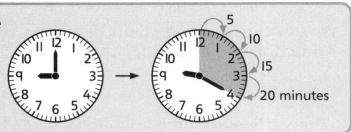

1. How many minutes is it past 9:00? Count by 5s.

a)

___25___ minutes

b)

_____ minutes

c)

_____ minutes

d)

_____ minutes

e)

_____ minutes

f)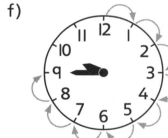

_____ minutes

2. Rob thinks that the time is 9:05 because the minute hand points to 5.

    Explain his mistake. _____

    _____

    _____

    _____

REMINDER ▶ The minute hand is the longer hand.

3. Circle the minute hand. Then count by 5s to write the minutes.

a) 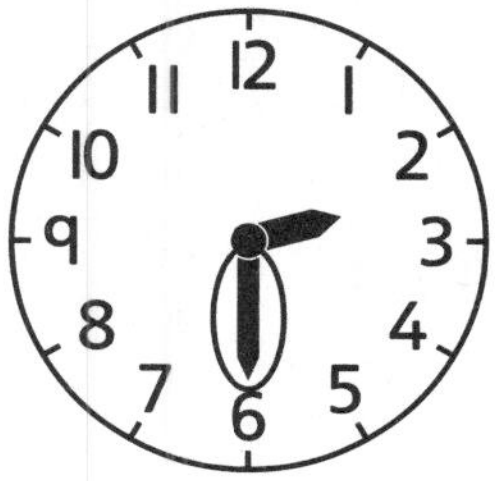

2 : 30

b) 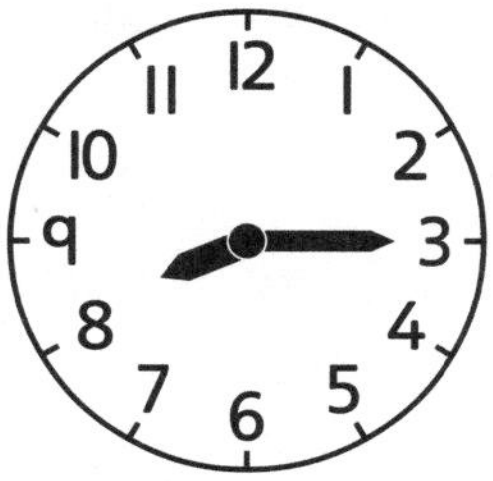

8 : ______

c) 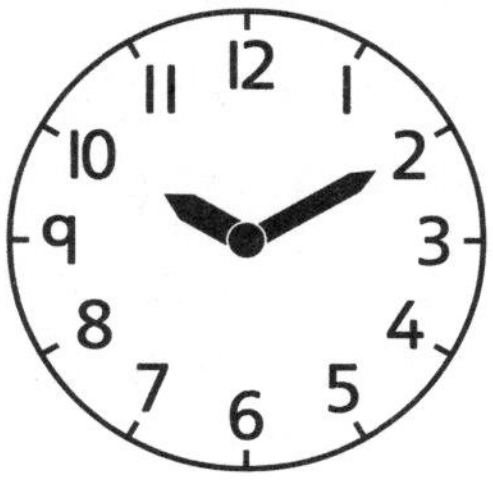

10 : ______

d) 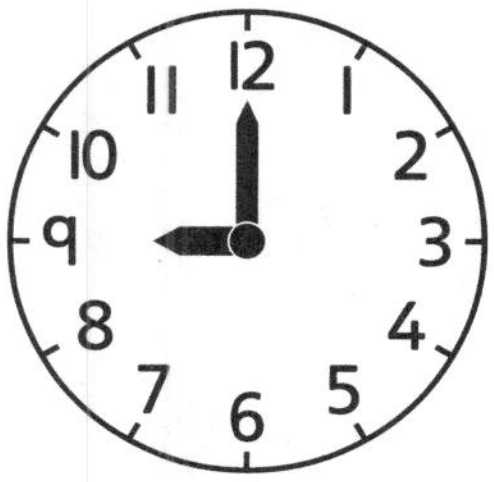

9 : ______

e) 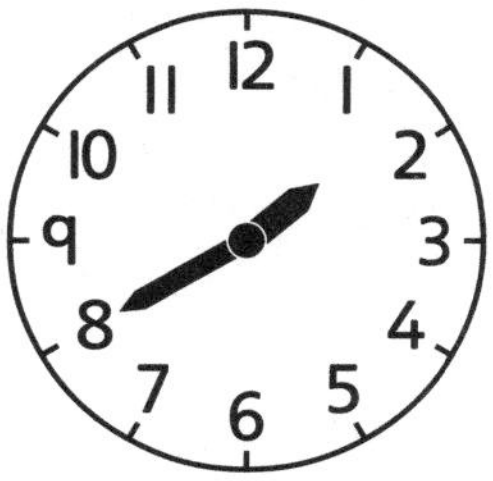

1 : ______

f) 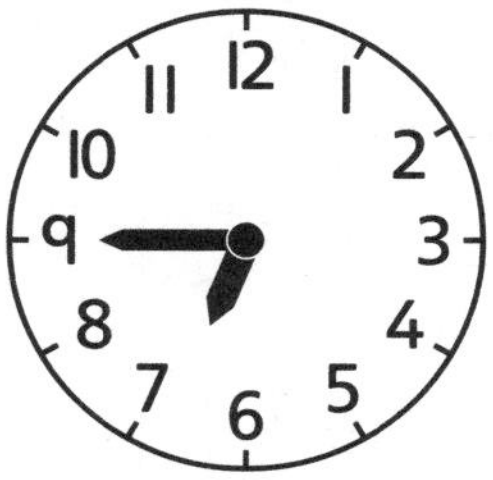

6 : ______

g) 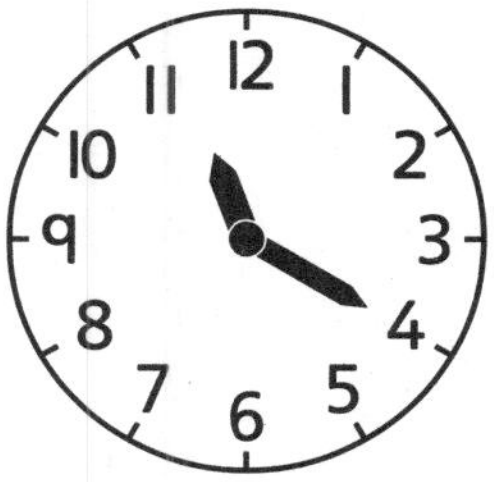

11 : ______

h) 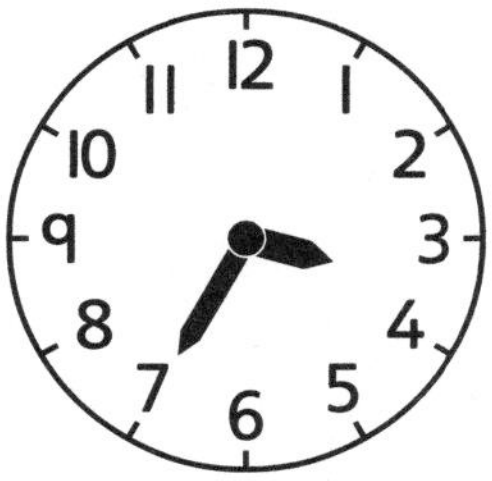

3 : ______

i) 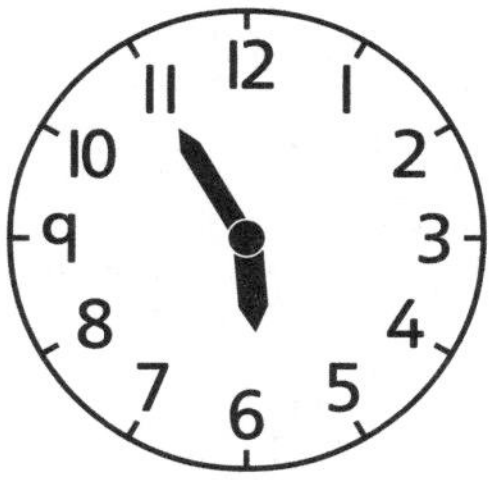

5 : ______

4. What time is it?

a) 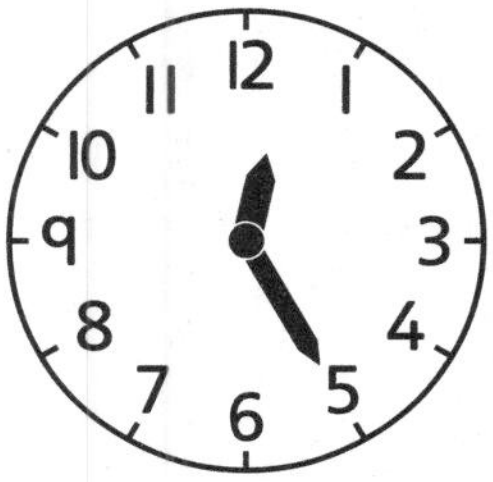

______ minutes past 12

b) 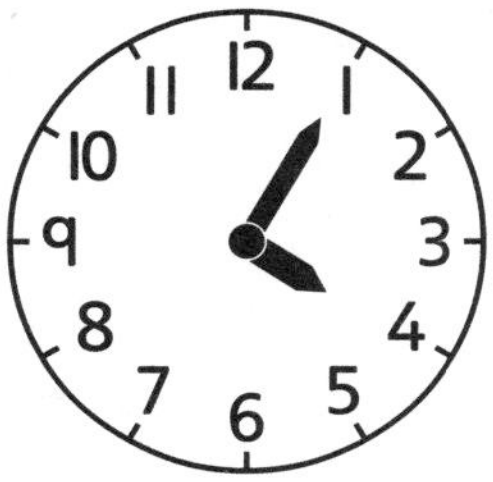

______ minutes past 4

c) 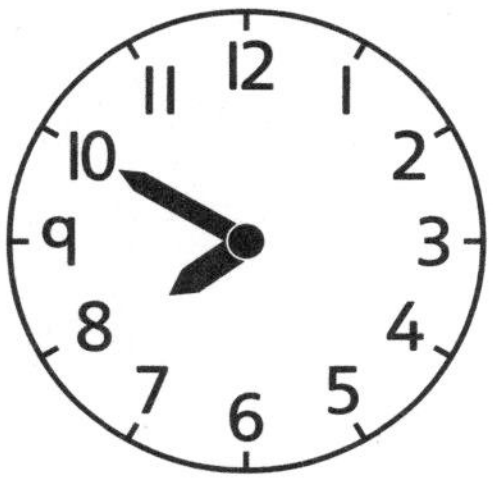

______ minutes past 7

The minute hand points at 3. Three times 5 minutes
have passed after 9:00.

3 × 5 = 15 minutes have passed. The time is 9:15.

5. Draw the arrows to show how the minute hand moved from 9:00.
Then write the multiplication equation.

a)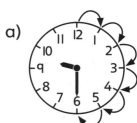

_____6 × 5 = 30_____

b)

_____

c)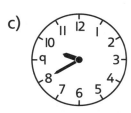

_____

d)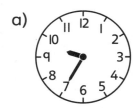

_____

e)

_____

f)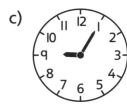

_____

6. Write a multiplication equation for the minutes passed after 9:00.
Then write the time.

a)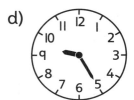

_____7 × 5 = 35_____

9 : ___35___

b)

_____

9 : _____

c)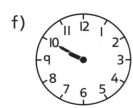

_____

9 : _____

BONUS ▶ The minute hand made one whole circle. How many
minutes passed? How do you know?

MD3-14 Time to the Five Minutes

What time is it?

Step 1: Look at the hour hand. It points between 4 and 5.
The hour is 4.

Step 2: Look at the minute hand. It points at 2. Skip count by 5s
or multiply by 5 to find the minutes: 5, 10 or 2 × 5 = 10.

The time is 4:10.

1. What time is it?

a)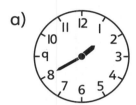

___1___ : ___40___

b)

_____ : _____

c)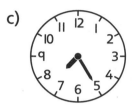

_____ : _____

d)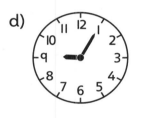

_____ : _____

e)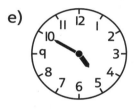

_____ : _____

f)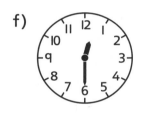

_____ : _____

2. Write the time on the digital clock.

a)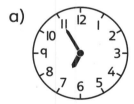

| 0 | 6 | : | 5 | 5 |

b)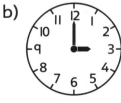

| | | : | | |

c)

| | | : | | |

d)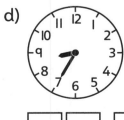

| | | : | | |

e)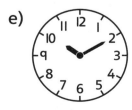

| | | : | | |

f)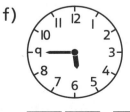

| | | : | | |

3. Write the time two ways.

a)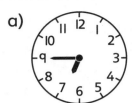

_____6:45_____

_____forty-five_____

_____minutes past six_____

b)

_____

_____

_____

c)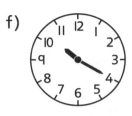

_____

_____

_____

d)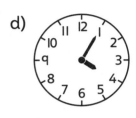

_____

_____

_____

e)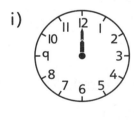

_____

_____

_____

f)

_____

_____

_____

g)

_____

_____

_____

h)

_____

_____

_____

i)

_____

_____

_____

BONUS ▶

a) Show the time 7:05 on the analog
and the digital clock.

b) Write the time two ways.

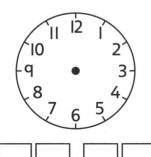

_____

_____

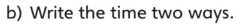

Measurement and Data 3-14

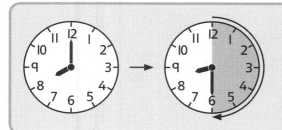

It is half an hour after 8:00.
The time is **half past** 8.

$6 \times 5 = 30$, so the time is 8:30.

1. Write the time two ways.

a)

half past _____

_____ : _____

b)

half past _____

_____ : _____

c)

half past _____

_____ : _____

d)

half past _____

_____ : _____

2. Write the time in numbers.

a) half past 8   b) half past 6   c) half past 10   d) half past 12

_____   _____   _____   _____

Some digital clocks do not show the first zero in the hours.
The clock shows half past 2.

3. Write the time in words and numbers.

a)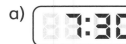

half past 7

b)

_____

c)

_____

d)

_____

e)

_____

f) 5:30

_____

4. What fraction of the circle is shaded?

a)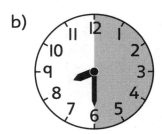

b)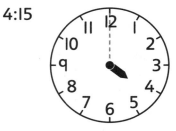

c)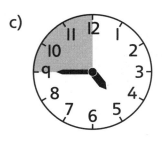

_____   _____   _____

5. a) Draw the minute hand on each clock. How much after the hour is it? Show by coloring.

7:15   4:15   12:15

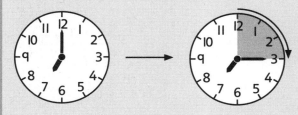      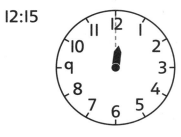

b) What part of the circles did you color? _____

c) What fraction of an hour is 15 minutes? _____

It is a quarter of an hour after 7:00 or **quarter past** 7.
$3 \times 5 = 15$, so the time is 7:15.

6. Write the time in words and numbers. Use "quarter" in your answer.

a)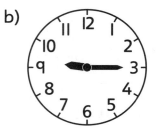

b)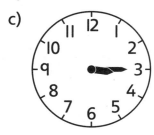

c)

_____   _____   _____

_____   _____   _____

7. Write the time in words. Use "half," "quarter," and "o'clock" when you can.

a)

fifty-five minutes

past six

b)

half past twelve

c)

d)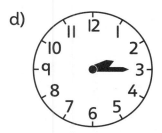

e)

f)

g) **11:00**

h) **10:35**

i) **1:20**

j) **5:15**

k) **4:30**

l) **8:03**

BONUS ▶ Write the time in as many ways as you can.

a)

b)

c)

On these clocks, all the minutes are marked. There are 60 minutes in 1 hour.

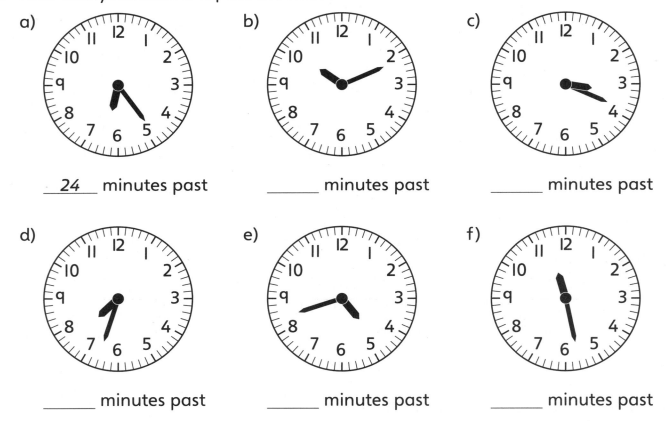

$4 \times 5 = 20$

2 more minutes passed

20 minutes past 7 or 7:20

22 minutes past 7, or 7:22

I. How many minutes is it past the hour?

a)

___24___ minutes past

b)

_____ minutes past

c)

_____ minutes past

d)

_____ minutes past

e)

_____ minutes past

f)

_____ minutes past

BONUS ▶ Look at the clock that shows 7:22 at the top of the page. An equation for the number of minutes for this clock is $(4 \times 5) + 2 = 22$.

Write an equation for the number of minutes in Question I.a).

_____

2. Write the exact time.

a)

 8 : 24

b)

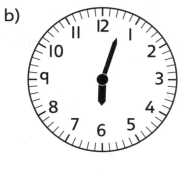

_____ : _____

c)

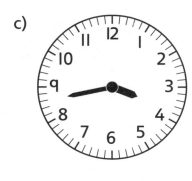

_____ : _____

d)

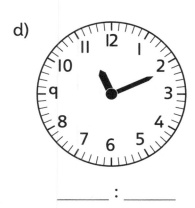

_____ : _____

e)

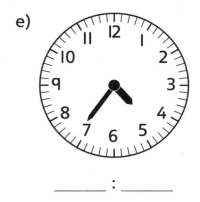

_____ : _____

f)

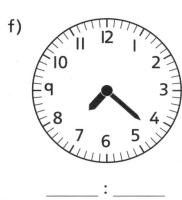

_____ : _____

BONUS ▶

g)

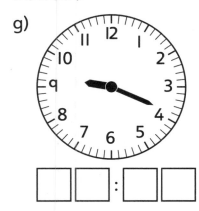

☐☐ : ☐☐

h)

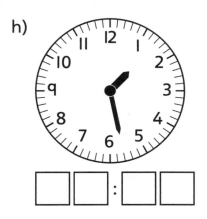

☐☐ : ☐☐

i)

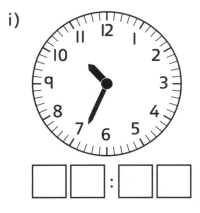

☐☐ : ☐☐

j)

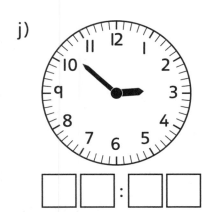

☐☐ : ☐☐

k)

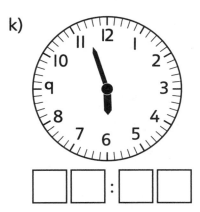

☐☐ : ☐☐

l)

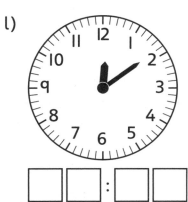

☐☐ : ☐☐

I. How much time passed from 8:00 to the time shown?

a)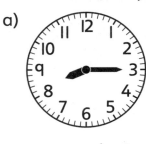

_____ minutes

b)

_____ minutes

c)

_____ minutes

2. Draw arrows to show how the minute hand moves from the start time to the end time.

a)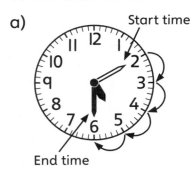

b)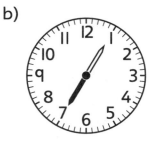

c)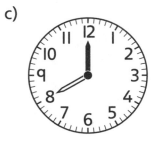

3. These clocks show only the minute hand, with white for the start time and black for the end. Count by 5s to find out how much time passed.

a)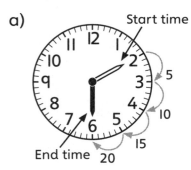

___20___ minutes

b)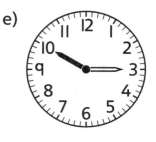

_____ minutes

c)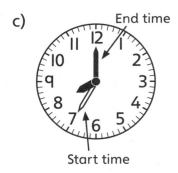

_____ minutes

d)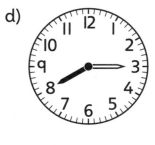

_____ minutes

e)

_____ minutes

f)

_____ minutes

4. Count by 5s to find out how much time passed.

a) 7:10 to 7:25

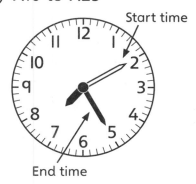

Start time

End time

____15 minutes____

b) 3:15 to 3:40

_____

c) 10:25 to 10:40

_____

d) 5:35 to 6:00

_____

e) 2:40 to 3:00

_____

f) 8:25 to 9:00

_____

g) 9:35 to 9:55

_____

h) 5:10 to 5:55

_____

BONUS ▶ 6:55 to 7:15

_____

5. Use a clock to solve the problem.

a) Tina played guitar from 5:10 to 5:45. How long did she play for?

b) Ethan read from 6:15 to 6:55. How long did he read for?

c) A TV show starts at 7:25 and ends at 8:00. How long is the show?

6. The clock shows the time when Grace started reading. She read for 20 minutes. When did she stop reading?

a)

Grace stopped at

_____5:30_____ .

b)

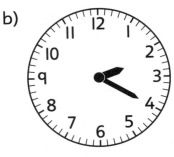

Grace stopped at

_____ .

c)

Grace stopped at

_____ .

BONUS ▶

d)

Grace stopped at

_____ .

e)

Grace stopped at

_____ .

f)

Grace stopped at

_____ .

7. Use a clock to solve the problem.

a) Tim went skating at 7:20. He skated for 25 minutes. When did he finish skating?

b) Anne started doing homework at 6:30. The homework took 30 minutes to finish. When did she finish her homework?

BONUS ▶

a) It takes Carl 3 minutes to read a page. He read 10 pages. How long did he read for?

b) He started reading at 7:45. When did he finish reading?

Measurement and Data 3-17

1. Count by 5s to find how much time passed.

   a) from 3:10 to 3:25

   _____

   b) from 5:30 to 5:55

   _____

   c) from 11:05 to 11:50

   _____

> 15 minutes passed from 3:10 to 3:25. We say that 15 minutes **elapsed**.

2. Find the elapsed time. Count by 5s and then count by 1s.

   a) from 3:15 to 3:32

   _____*17 minutes*_____

   b) from 5:10 to 5:23

   _____

   c) from 6:05 to 6:22

   _____

   d) from 8:20 to 8:38

   _____

   e) from 9:30 to 9:43

   _____

   BONUS ▶ from 12:55 to 1:21

   _____

How much time has passed from 2:30 to 2:50?

Zara counts by 5s.

| 2:30 | 2:35 | 2:40 | 2:45 | 2:50 |

Zara has 4 fingers up for 2:50. $4 \times 5 = 20$, so 20 minutes passed.

3. Count by 5s from the start time. How many fingers are up?
   Write the multiplication equation.

   a) from 2:20 to 2:55

   __7__ fingers are up

   __7__ × 5 = __35__

   b) from 7:15 to 7:25

   _____ fingers are up

   _____ × 5 = _____

   c) from 10:40 to 10:50

   _____ fingers are up

   _____ × 5 = _____

   d) from 8:15 to 8:55

   _____ fingers are up

   _____ × 5 = _____

   e) from 12:10 to 12:55

   _____ fingers are up

   _____ × 5 = _____

   f) from 5:40 to 6:00

   _____ fingers are up

   _____ × 5 = _____

4. Count by 5s to find the elapsed time.

   a) from 3:10 to 3:25

   _____

   b) from 6:15 to 6:40

   _____

   c) from 9:35 to 10:00

   _____

   d) from 11:00 to 11:25

   _____

   e) from 1:25 to 1:55

   _____

   BONUS ▶ from 4:55 to 5:10

   _____

5. Ivan went to the Natural History Museum. How much time
   did he spend in each section?

Section	Start Time	End Time	Elapsed Time
Ocean Hall	10:05	10:25	
Mammals	10:25	10:55	

How much time passed from 2:35 to 2:37?

Mike counts by 1s:

2:35   2:36   2:37

Bev says: "The hours are the same. Only the minutes changed. I can subtract 37 − 35 = 2. So, 2 minutes passed."

Mike has 2 fingers up for 2:37.

So, 2 minutes passed.

1. How much time passed? Count by 1s or subtract.

   a) from 3:10 to 3:13   b) from 6:15 to 6:17   c) from 9:35 to 9:39

   _____   _____   _____

   d) from 11:00 to 11:04   e) from 1:25 to 1:26   f) from 4:55 to 4:58

   _____   _____   _____

How much time has passed from 2:30 to 2:53?

Jin counts by 5s from 2:30 to 2:50. He counts by 1s from 2:50 to 2:53.

Jin draws a picture to keep track.

   20 minutes   + 3 minutes = 23 minutes passed

2:30   2:50   2:53

2. Use Jin's method to find the elapsed time.

   a) from 3:20 to 3:47

   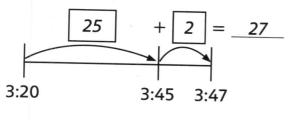

   $\boxed{25}$ + $\boxed{2}$ = __27__

   3:20   3:45   3:47

   __27__ minutes passed

   b) from 5:05 to 5:33

   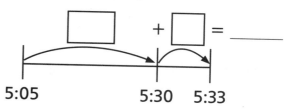

   $\boxed{}$ + $\boxed{}$ = _____

   5:05   5:30   5:33

   _____ minutes passed

3. Finish the picture and find the elapsed time.

a) from 8:10 to 8:28

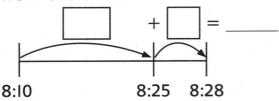

☐ + ☐ = _____

8:10   8:25   8:28

b) from 10:25 to 10:56

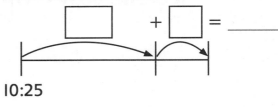

☐ + ☐ = _____

10:25

_____   _____

c) from 12:15 to 12:54

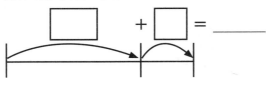

☐ + ☐ = _____

_____   _____   _____

d) from 5:45 to 6:01

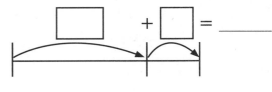

☐ + ☐ = _____

_____   _____   _____

BONUS ▶ from 9:04 to 9:42

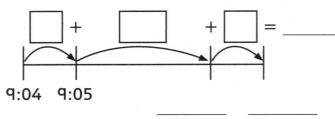

☐ + ☐ + ☐ = _____

9:04   9:05

_____   _____

4. Sara ran for 3 minutes. When did she finish running?

a) Sara started at 2:30.   b) Sara started at 5:20.   c) Sara started at 12:15.

She finished at _____.   She finished at _____.   She finished at _____.

5. Don talked on the phone. When did he finish talking?

a) Don started at 3:25 and talked for 5 minutes. _____

b) Don started at 8:30 and talked for 8 minutes. _____

c) Don started at 9:35 and talked for 12 minutes. _____

6. A plane left San Diego, CA, at 5:05. It landed at Los Angeles, CA, at 5:52. How long was the flight?

MD3-20 Timelines

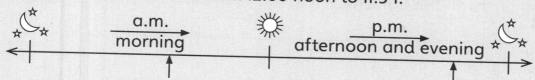
1. Write "a.m." or "p.m."

   a) Lily eats breakfast at 7:30 _____   b) Ray goes to school at 8:15 _____

   c) School ends at 3:35 _____   d) Dinner is at 5:30 _____

   e) Karate class starts at 5:45 _____   f) The math test starts at 9:15 _____

2. Write the time. Use "a.m." or "p.m."

   a) The morning TV show starts   b) The bedtime story ends

   at ___6:45 a.m.___   at _____

   c) Hanna eats lunch at _____   d) Anwar gets to school at _____

   e) Half past 8 in the morning   f) Quarter past 5 in the evening

   is _____   is _____

BONUS ▶

g) 3 hours before noon is _____   h) 12 minutes after midnight is _____

3. Fill in the missing times on the timeline.

a)

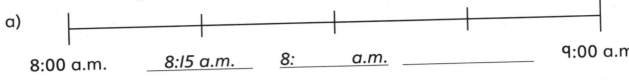

8:00 a.m.   _8:15 a.m._   _8:____ a.m._   _____   9:00 a.m.

b)

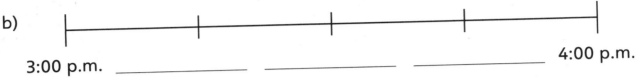

3:00 p.m.   _____   _____   _____   4:00 p.m.

4. The timeline shows what Peter does after school.

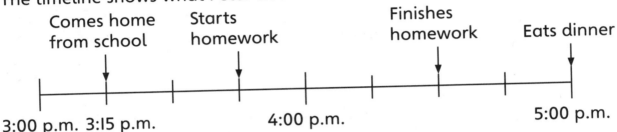

a) Use Peter's timeline to fill in the table. Use "a.m." and "p.m."

	Comes home from school	Starts homework	Finishes homework
Time			

b) How much time does homework take? _____

c) How much time does Peter have between homework and dinner? _____

d) Peter's dad comes home from work 15 minutes before dinner.

   At what time does Peter's dad come home? _____

   Show this time on the timeline.

e) Is each elapsed time more than 1 hour? Circle the answer.

   from coming home to eating dinner   more   less

   from starting homework to eating dinner   more   less

   from 3:00 p.m. to starting homework   more   less

f) How does a timeline help you to answer part e)?

MD3-21 Adding Time

You can write elapsed time the same way you write hours of the day, with a colon (:), but without "a.m." and "p.m."

Example: noon to 6:00 p.m. = 6 hours = 6:00

1. Write the elapsed time using a colon.

a) 45 minutes

    __0:45__

b) 2 hours 3 minutes

    __2:03__

c) 3 hours 15 minutes

    _____

d) 10 hours 12 minutes

    _____

e) 4 hours 9 minutes

    _____

f) 32 minutes

    _____

g) 5 minutes

    _____

h) 3 hours

    _____

BONUS ▶ 13 hours

    _____

Kathy started reading at 1:05 p.m. She read for 32 minutes.
When did she finish reading?

1	:	0	5	← Start time
+ 0	:	3	2	← Elapsed time = 32 minutes = 0 hours 32 minutes = 0:32
1	:	3	7	

Kathy finished reading at 1:37 p.m.

---

2. Add to find the end time.

a)
2	:	1	5
+ 0	:	2	1
	:		

b)
3	:	2	1
+ 1	:	3	4
	:		

c)
1 0	:	1	6
+	1	:	2	1
		:		

d)
2	:	1	5
+ 6	:	3	0
	:		

e)
8	:	2	4
+ 1	:	0	7
	:		

f)
1 1	:	1	6
+	0	:	4	3
		:		

3. Add the times to solve.

a) Nina played soccer for 45 minutes. She started at 6:05 p.m. When did she finish playing?

6	:	0	5
+ 0	:	4	5
	:		

Nina finished playing at _____.

b) Jay put bread in the oven at 4:25 p.m. The bread has to bake for 22 minutes. When will the bread be ready?

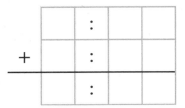

The bread will be ready at _____.

c) An art class is 1 hour and 30 minutes long. It starts at 10:15 a.m. When does the art class end?

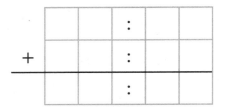

The art class ends at _____.

d) Jen left home at 8:43 a.m. It takes her 12 minutes to get to school. When did she get to school?

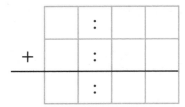

Jen got to school at _____.

e) A birthday party starts at 3:20 p.m. and lasts for 2 hours and 30 minutes. When does the party end?

f) Glen set out from Washington, DC, at 3:25 p.m. It took him 1 hour and 19 minutes to get to Baltimore, MD. When did he arrive in Baltimore?

BONUS ▶

a) It takes Mindy 2 minutes to serve 1 person at a coffee shop. How much time does it take her to serve 25 people?

b) Mindy started her morning shift at 9:05 a.m. She served 25 people before a break. When did she take the break?

MD3-22 Subtracting Time

1. Write the elapsed time in hours and minutes.

a) 0:04 = ___0___ hours ___4___ minutes   b) 0:35 = _____ hours _____ minutes

c) 2:14 = _____ hours _____ minutes   d) 4:06 = _____ hours _____ minutes

e) 10:30 = _____ hours _____ minutes f) 0:05 = _____ hours _____ minutes

A swimming lesson started at 1:05 p.m. It ended at 1:45 p.m. How long
did it last for?

	1	:	4	5	← End time
−	1	:	0	5	← Start time
	0	:	4	0	← Elapsed time = 0 hours 40 minutes

The swimming lesson lasted for 40 minutes.

2. Subtract to find the elapsed time. Write the answer in words and numbers.

a)

	2	:	4	5
−	1	:	2	1
		:		

_____ hour

_____ minutes

b)

	3	:	2	1
−	1	:	1	1
		:		

_____ hours

_____ minutes

c)

	1	0	:	3	6
−		2	:	2	3
			:		

_____ hours

_____ minutes

d)

	6	:	4	5
−	6	:	3	2
		:		

_____ hours

_____ minutes

e)

	8	:	2	9
−	8	:	2	1
		:		

_____ hours

_____ minutes

f)

	1	1	:	5	1
−		2	:	5	1
			:		

_____ hours

_____ minutes

3. Subtract the time to solve the problem.

a) Tasha played baseball from 4:26 p.m. to 4:45 p.m. How long did she play for?

4	:	4	5
−	:		
	:		

Tasha played for _____.

b) Alex started homework at 7:05 p.m. and finished it at 7:52 p.m. How long did he spend on homework?

7	:	5	2
−	:		
	:		

Alex spent _____.

c) A judo class starts at 4:20 p.m. and ends at 4:55 p.m. How long does it last?

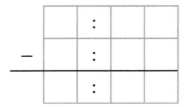

The judo class lasts _____.

d) A movie starts at 9:05 a.m. on Saturday and ends at 10:53 a.m. How long is the movie?

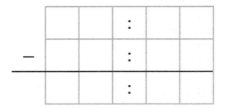

The movie lasts _____.

e) A birthday party starts at 3:20 p.m. and ends at 4:30 p.m. How long is the party?

f) A soccer match lasts from 5:01 p.m. to 6:49 p.m. How long is the match?

BONUS ▶

The picture shows Karen's clock at home when she leaves for school and the clock at school when she gets to school.

a) Where is each clock? Write "school" or "home."

_____

b) How long does it take Karen to get to school?

_____

MD3-23 Telling Time (Advanced)

The hour hand is between 6 and 7.

How many minutes are left before 7 o'clock?

The minute hand is between 8 and 9.

Count by 5s to get from 12 to 9. Then count by 1s.

15 + 2 = 17, so the time is 17 minutes to 7.

I. What time is it?

a)

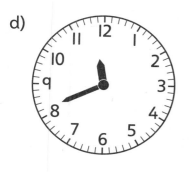

_____ minutes to 7

b)

_____ minutes to 10

c)

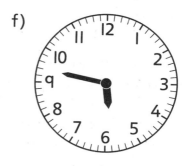

_____ minutes to 4

d)

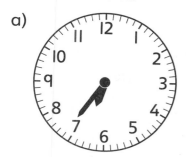

_____ minutes to _____

e)

_____ minutes to _____

f)

_____ minutes to _____

g)

_____ minutes to _____

h)

_____ minutes to _____

i)

_____ minutes to _____

2. Tell the time two ways, as minutes past the hour and minutes
to the next hour.

a)

_____ minutes past _____

_____ minutes to _____

b)

_____ minutes past _____

_____ minutes to _____

c)

_____ minutes past _____

_____ minutes to _____

d)

_____ minutes past _____

_____ minutes to _____

It is 4:40. How much time is left before 5 o'clock?
There are 60 minutes in 1 hour. 40 minutes passed after 4:00.

60 − 40 = 20 minutes left

The time is 20 minutes to 5.

3. How many minutes are left before 5 o'clock? Write the subtraction equation.

a) 4:37

60 − ___37___

= ___23___

b) 4:05

60 − _____

= _____

c) 4:50

60 − _____

= _____

d) 4:58

60 − _____

= _____

e)

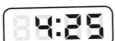 4:25

_____

f)

 4:45

_____

g)

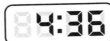 4:36

_____

h)

 4:41

_____

4. Tell the time two ways.

a)

_____ minutes past _____

_____ minutes to _____

b)

_____ minutes past _____

_____ minutes to _____

c)

_____ minutes past _____

_____ minutes to _____

d) 4:16

_____ minutes past _____

_____ minutes to _____

Three quarters of an hour passed after 4:00. One quarter of an hour is left before 5:00.

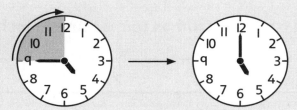

The time is **quarter to** 5.

5. What time is it? Use "quarter to" in your answer.

a)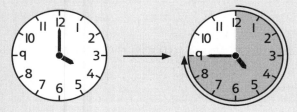

_____quarter to 1_____

b)

_____

c)

_____

d) 1:45

e) 04:45

f) 7:45

6. Write the time in words in as many ways as you can.

a) 6:12   b) 7:15   c) 3:00   d) 12:45   e) 10:30   f) 2:35

MD3-24 Inches

An **inch (in)** is a unit for measuring length.
Two fingers measure about 1 inch across.

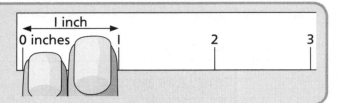

1. Use two fingers to estimate the length in inches.

   a) My pencil is about _____ inches long.

   b) My eraser is about _____ inches long.

   c) My JUMP Math book is about _____ inches long.

   d) My shoe is about _____ inches wide.

   e) My desk is about _____ inches wide.

You can count jumps to measure in inches.

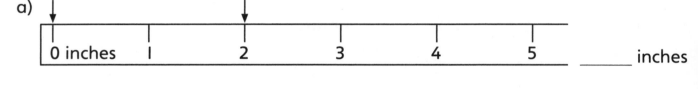

4 jumps = 4 inches

2. Measure the distance between the arrows.

   a)

   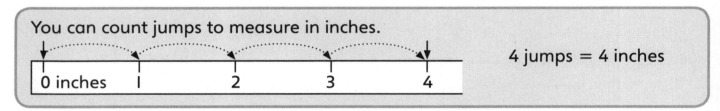

   _____ inches

   b)

   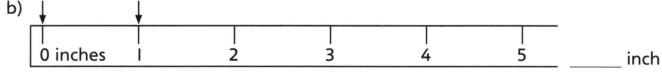

   _____ inch

   c)

   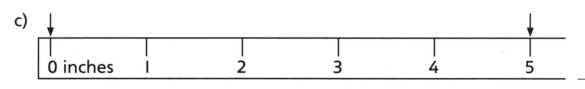

   _____ inches

BONUS ▶

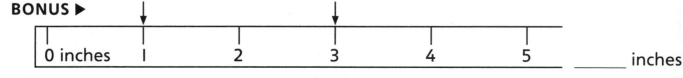

_____ inches

3. Measure the length of the line or object. Write "in" for inches.

a)
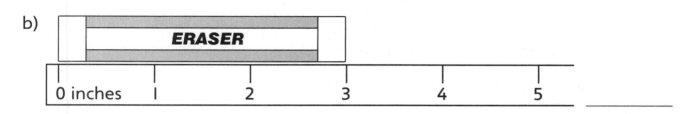
0 inches   1   2   3   4   5   _4 in_

b)

0 inches   1   2   3   4   5   _____

c)
0 inches   1   2   3   4   5   _____

4. Use a ruler to measure the length of the line or object.

a)  _____ _in_

b)  _____

c)  _____

d)
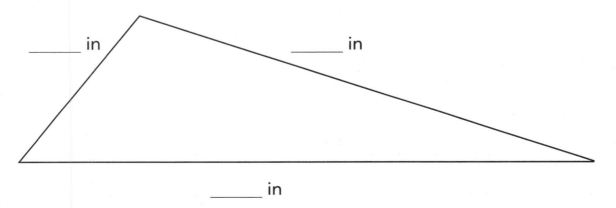
_____

5. Measure the length of each side of the triangle.

_____ in   _____ in

_____ in

6. Draw two arrows on the ruler that are the given distance apart. Start at the "0" mark.

a) 2 inches

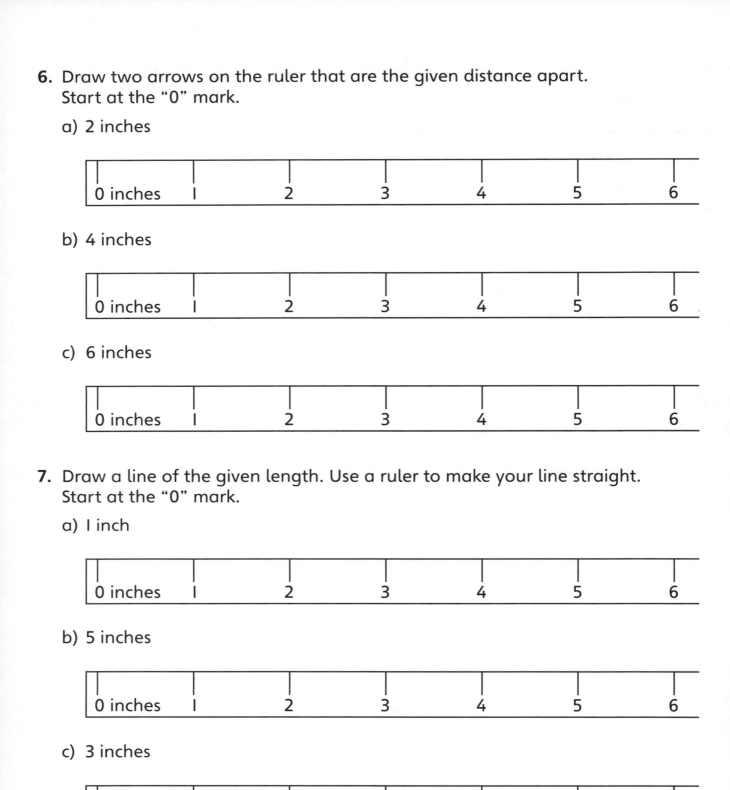

b) 4 inches

c) 6 inches

7. Draw a line of the given length. Use a ruler to make your line straight. Start at the "0" mark.

a) I inch

b) 5 inches

c) 3 inches

8. Use a ruler to draw a line of the given length.

a) 3 inches   b) 2 inches   c) 6 inches

I. Write the missing fractions or mixed numbers on the number line.

a)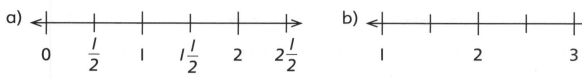

b)

c)

d)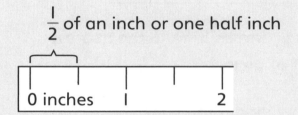

BONUS ▶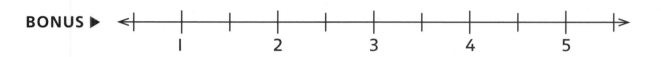

On this ruler, each inch is divided into 2 halves.

$\frac{1}{2}$ of an inch or one half inch

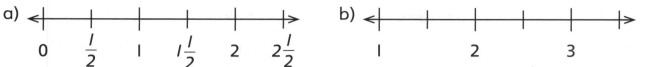

2. How long is the line?

a)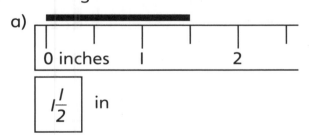

$1\frac{1}{2}$ in

b)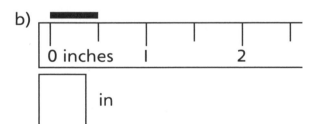

☐ in

c)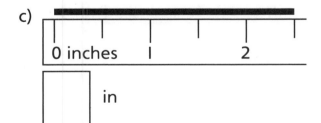

☐ in

d)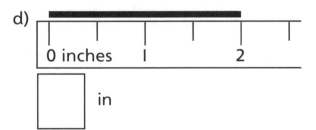

☐ in

e)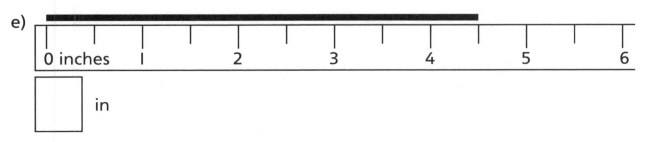

☐ in

3. Write the length.

a)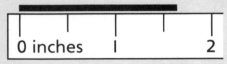

0 inches   1   2

☐ in

b)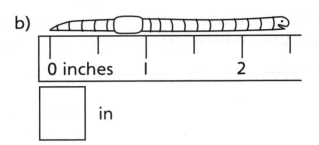

0 inches   1   2

☐ in

This line is about $1\frac{1}{2}$ inches long.

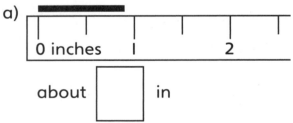

0 inches   1   2

It is $1\frac{1}{2}$ inches long to the nearest half of an inch.

This line is about 2 inches long.

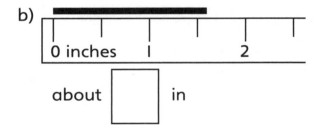

0 inches   1   2

It is 2 inches long to the nearest half of an inch.

---

4. How long is the line?

a)

0 inches   1   2

about ☐ in

b)

0 inches   1   2

about ☐ in

c)

0 inches   1   2

about ☐ in

d)

0 inches   1   2

about ☐ in

---

5. Measure the line to the nearest half of an inch.
Use a ruler with half-inch markings.

a) ▬▬▬▬▬   b) ▮   c) ▬▬▬   d) ╱

about ☐ in   about ☐ in   about ☐ in   about ☐ in

MD3-26 Quarters of an Inch

I. Write the missing mixed numbers on the number line.
Use the smallest denominator you can.

a)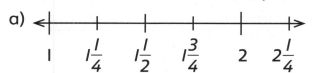

b)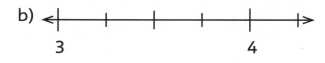

c)

d)

e)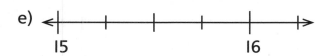

f)

BONUS ▶

2. Circle where the given mixed number or fraction belongs on the number line.

a) $1\frac{3}{4}$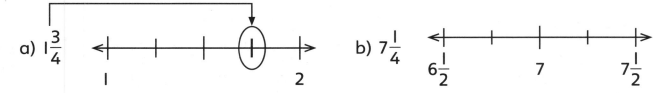

b) $7\frac{1}{4}$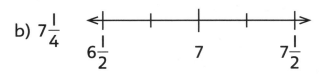

c) $6\frac{1}{4}$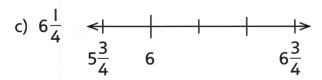

d) $\frac{3}{4}$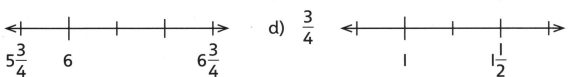

e) $9\frac{1}{2}$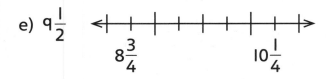

f) $7\frac{3}{4}$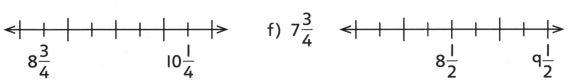

g) $\frac{1}{2}$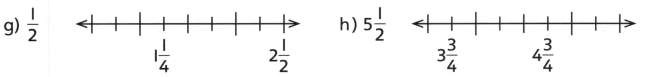

h) $5\frac{1}{2}$

On this ruler, each inch is divided into 4 quarters.

$\frac{1}{4}$ of an inch or one quarter inch

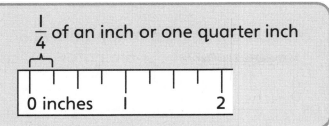

0 inches   1   2

3. How long is the line?

a)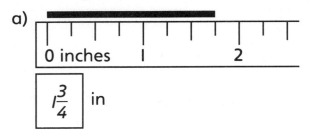

0 inches   1   2

$1\frac{3}{4}$ in

b)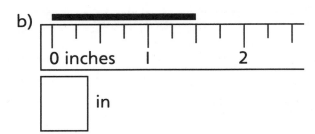

0 inches   1   2

☐ in

c)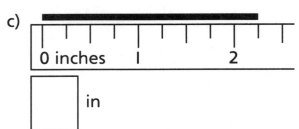

0 inches   1   2

☐ in

d)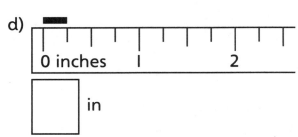

0 inches   1   2

☐ in

4. What is the length of the object?

a)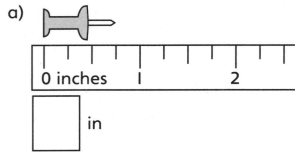

0 inches   1   2

☐ in

b)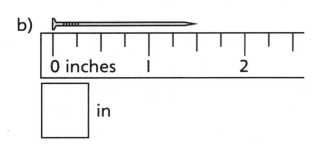

0 inches   1   2

☐ in

c)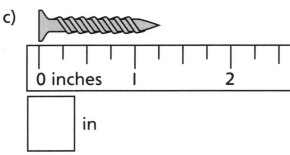

0 inches   1   2

☐ in

d)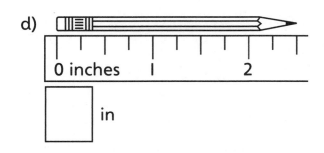

0 inches   1   2

☐ in

This line is about $1\frac{1}{4}$ inches long.

| 0 inches | I | | 2 |

It is $1\frac{1}{4}$ inches long to the nearest quarter of an inch.

This line is about I inch long.

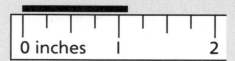

| 0 inches | I | | 2 |

It is I inch long to the nearest quarter of an inch.

5. What is the length of the line to the nearest quarter of an inch?

a)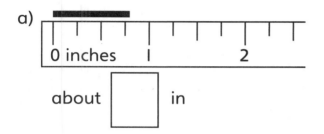

about [ ] in

b)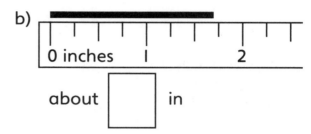

about [ ] in

c)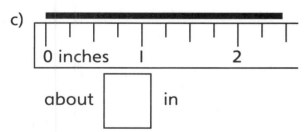

about [ ] in

d)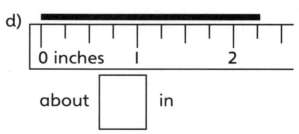

about [ ] in

6. Measure to the nearest quarter of an inch. Use a ruler with quarter-inch markings.

a)

about [ ] in

b)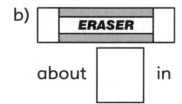

about [ ] in

c)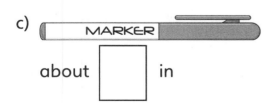

about [ ] in

d)

about [ ] in

I. Measure the heights of the flowers to the nearest quarter of an inch.

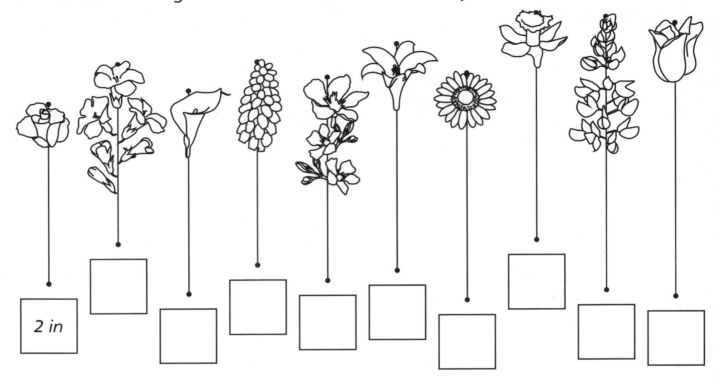

2 in

We can show measurements using a **line plot**.

This is a line plot for Question I.

Heights of Flowers ← title

← number line

2   2¼   2½   2¾   3

Height (inches) ← label

2. Look at the line plot above.

a) How many flowers are 2 inches tall? _____

b) How many ✕s are shown for 2 inches? _____

c) How many flowers are 2¼ inches tall? _____

d) How many ✕s are shown for 2¼ inches? _____

BONUS ▶ How many flowers are 2¾ inches tall? _____

3. a) Measure the lengths of the worms to the nearest quarter of an inch.

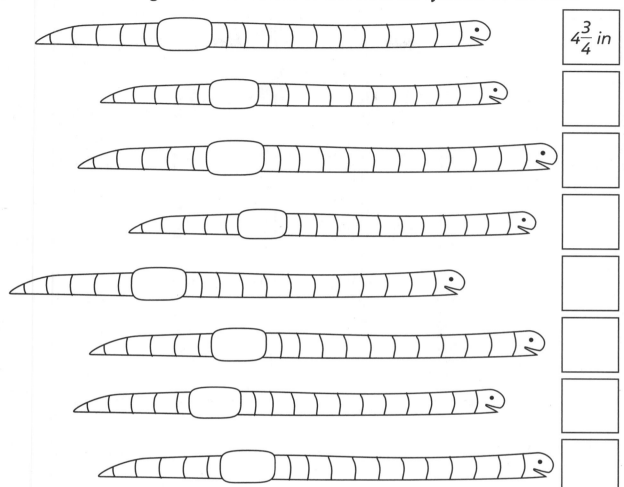

$4\frac{3}{4}$ in

b) Underline the title of the line plot below.

c) Draw a box around the label. What units are used for measuring

the lengths? _____

d) Draw an ✗ on the line plot for each worm's length. Cross out each length after you draw an ✗ for it on the line plot.

e) How many worms are $4\frac{3}{4}$ inches long? _____

f) How many worms are 5 inches long? _____

Lengths of Worms

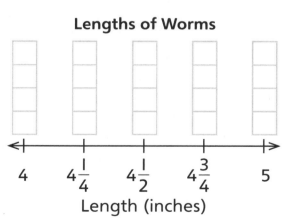

4     $4\frac{1}{4}$ $4\frac{1}{2}$ $4\frac{3}{4}$ 5

Length (inches)

4. a) Measure the lengths of the pencils to the nearest quarter of an inch.

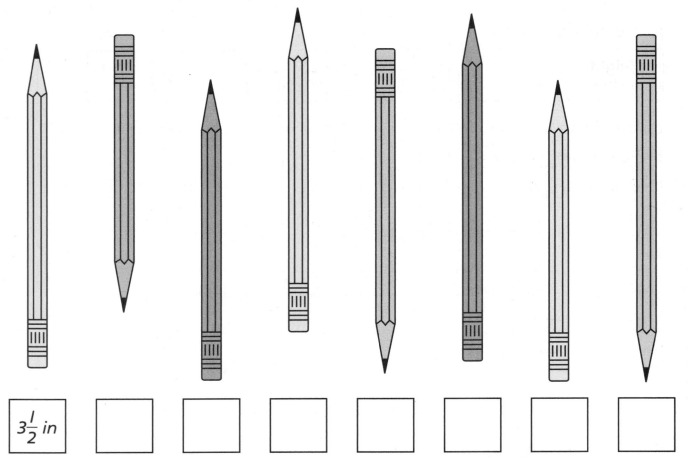

$3\frac{1}{2}$ in							

b) What is the title of the line plot below? _____

What is the label? _____

c) Draw an ✗ on the line plot for each pencil's length. Cross out each length after you draw an ✗ for it on the line plot.

Lengths of Pencils

d) How many pencils are $3\frac{1}{2}$ inches long? _____

e) How many pencils are $3\frac{1}{4}$ inches long? _____

Length (inches)

BONUS ▶ How many pencils are 4 inches long? _____

MD3-28 Creating Line Plots

1. The students in Mary's class measure the heights of 10 bamboo shoots to the nearest quarter of an inch. Mary records the heights in a table.

Height (inches)	13	13	$13\frac{1}{4}$	$13\frac{1}{4}$	$13\frac{1}{4}$	$13\frac{3}{4}$	$13\frac{3}{4}$	14	$14\frac{1}{4}$	$14\frac{1}{4}$

a) Underline the title of the line plot below. Draw a box around the label.

b) Finish the number line for the line plot.

c) Draw an ✗ in the line plot for each of the heights in Mary's table. Cross out each height after you draw an ✗ for it in the line plot.

Heights of Bamboo Shoots

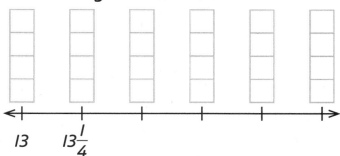

Height (inches)

d) Fill in the blanks to check your work for part c).

Number of bamboo shoots of height $13\frac{3}{4}$ inches _____

Number of ✗s in the line plot for $13\frac{3}{4}$ inches _____

Number of bamboo shoots of height $14\frac{1}{4}$ inches _____

Number of ✗s in the line plot for $14\frac{1}{4}$ inches _____

Total number of bamboo shoots _____

Total number of ✗s _____

BONUS ▶ How many bamboo shoots are less than 14 inches tall? _____

BONUS ▶ How many bamboo shoots are more than $13\frac{1}{4}$ inches tall and less than $14\frac{1}{4}$ inches tall? _____

2. The table shows the lengths of 12 different pencils.

Length (inches)	$5\frac{1}{2}$	5	$5\frac{1}{4}$	$5\frac{3}{4}$	$5\frac{3}{4}$	5	$6\frac{1}{4}$	$5\frac{3}{4}$	$5\frac{1}{4}$	$5\frac{1}{2}$	$5\frac{1}{4}$	$5\frac{1}{4}$

a) What is the title of the line plot below? _____

What is the label? _____

b) Finish the number line for the line plot.

c) Draw an ✗ on the line plot for each of the lengths in the table above. Cross out each length after you draw an ✗ for it on the line plot.

Lengths of Pencils

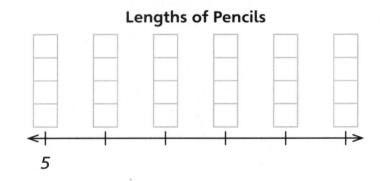

Length (inches)

d) Use the line plot above to answer the questions.

How many pencils are 6 inches long? _____

How many pencils are longer than 6 inches? _____

How many pencils are $5\frac{1}{2}$ inches long? _____

How many pencils are shorter than $5\frac{1}{2}$ inches? _____

How many more pencils are $5\frac{1}{4}$ inches long than $5\frac{1}{2}$ inches long? _____

Are most of the pencils longer or shorter than 6 inches? _____

Explain. _____

BONUS ▶ How many pencils are more than 5 inches long and less than $5\frac{3}{4}$ inches long? _____

       Measurement and Data 3-28

3. a) Measure the lengths of the paper clips to the nearest quarter of an inch.

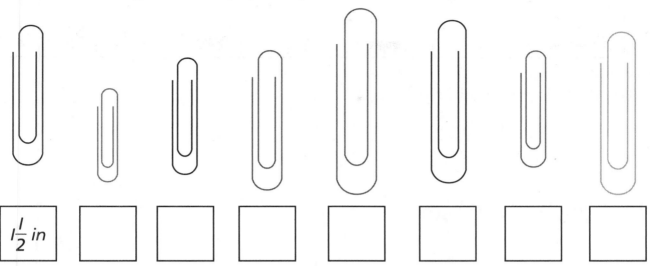

$1\frac{1}{2}$ in

b) The line plot below will show the measurements of the paper clips. Write a title for the line plot in the space provided.

c) Write a label for the line plot in the space provided.

d) Find the shortest length of the paper clips. Write that number at the start of the number line.

e) Complete the number line.

f) Complete the line plot to show the paper clip lengths. Cross out each length after you draw an ✗ for it on the line plot.

Title: _____

Label: _____

BONUS ▶ How many paper clips are more than $1\frac{1}{4}$ inches long and

less than 2 inches long? _____

MD3-29 Feet and Yards

A **foot** is another unit for measuring length.

Your arm from your elbow to your fingertips is about 1 foot long. One foot or more **feet** can be written with the short form "**ft.**"

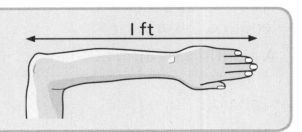

1 ft

1. Circle the things that are more than 1 foot long. Cross out the things that are less than 1 foot long.

There are 12 inches in 1 foot. You can measure in feet using a foot-long ruler.

1 foot

| inches | 1 | 2 | 3 | 4 | 5 | 6 | 7 | 8 | 9 | 10 | 11 | 12 |

2. Estimate with your arm. Then measure to the nearest foot.

		Estimate	Measurement
a)	The width of your desk		
b)	The length of a table		
c)	The width of a window		
d)	The length of a blackboard		

3. Circle the unit you would use to measure the height.

a)
(inch)
foot

b)
inch
foot

c)
inch
foot

d)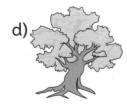
inch
foot

A **yard (yd)** is a unit for measuring length or distance.

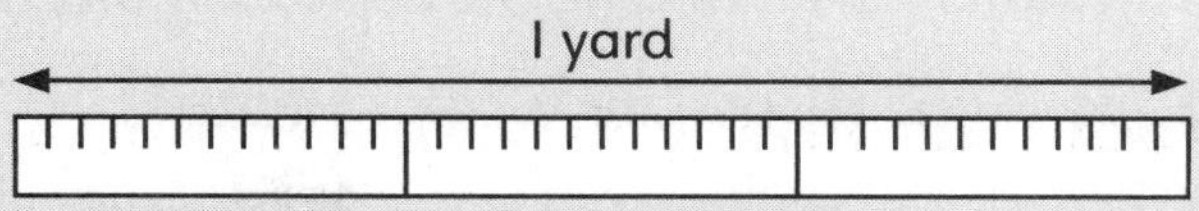

I yard

A giant step is about I yd long. This picture shows that a **yardstick** is I yard long.

4. Estimate using giant steps. Then measure using a yardstick or measuring tape.

		Estimate	Measurement
a)	The width of your classroom		
b)	The length of your classroom		
c)	The distance from your chair to the door		
d)	The width of the hallway		
e)	The length of the hallway		

There are 3 feet in I yard.

I yard = 3 feet   I yd = 3 ft

5. a) Fill in the measurements in feet.

yd	I	2	3	4	5	6	7	8
ft	3							

b) To change a measurement from yards to feet,

what number do you multiply by? _____

Explain. _____

6. Ravi's backyard is 9 yards long.

a) What is the length of Ravi's backyard in feet?

b) Ben's backyard is 30 feet long. How much longer is Ben's backyard than Ravi's?

7. Lily walks 234 yards on Saturday. She walks 179 yards on Sunday.

    a) How far does Lily walk in total?

    b) How much farther does Lily walk on Saturday than on Sunday?

8. Will has 5 cans of soup. Each can is 4 inches high. He stacks them to make a tower.

    a) How tall is Will's tower?

    b) Grace adds 3 cans of the same size to the tower. How tall is the tower now?

9. Zara's swimming pool is 10 yards wide. She swims from one side to the other 8 times. How many yards does she swim?

    BONUS ▶ How much is this distance in feet?

10. A fence is made of 6 sections.

    a) If each section of the fence is 3 ft long, how long is the fence altogether?

    b) If the fence is 30 ft long, how long is each section?

11. Josh's bike is 2 yards long. He can fit 4 bikes of this length along a fence. How long is the fence in feet?

12. Tasha skates on an ice rink that is 9 yards wide. She skates from side to side 8 times.

    a) How many yards does Tasha skate?

    b) Sal skates from side to side 6 times. How much farther does Tasha skate?

A square with sides 1 inch long is called a **square inch**.

You can write square inch as **in²** for short.

You can measure area in square inches.

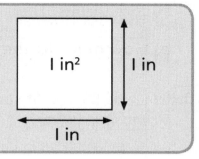

1. Count the number of square inches to find the area.

a)

Area = _____ in²

b)

Area = _____ in²

c)

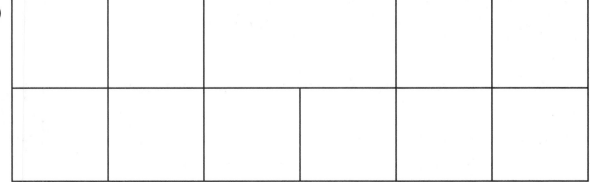

Area = _____ in²

2. Use a ruler to join the marks and divide the rectangle into square inches. Then find the area.

a)

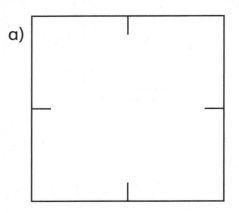

b)

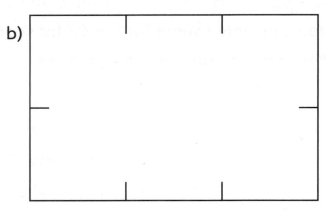

Area = _____ in²   Area = _____

3. Each grid square is I in². Find the areas of the shapes in square inches.

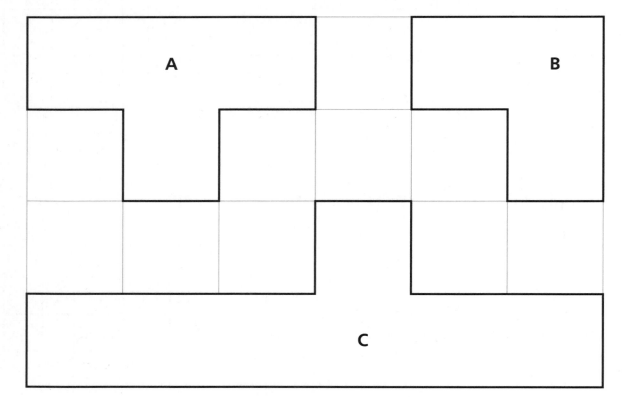

Area of A = _____ in²

Area of B = _____

Area of C = _____

MD3-3I Area in Square Feet and Square Yards

A square with sides I foot long is called a **square foot**.

You can write square foot as **ft²** for short.

You can measure area in square feet.

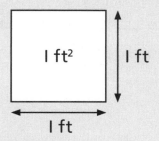

This is a picture of a square foot.

I. Each small square is a picture of I ft². Find the area of the larger shape.

a)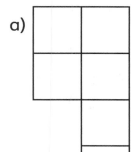

Area = _____ ft²

b)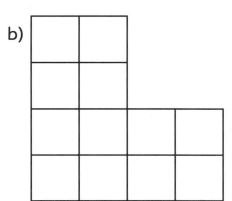

Area = _____

c)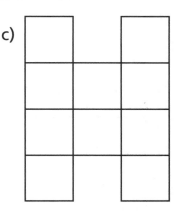

Area = _____

2. Yu puts tiles on her bathroom floor, as shown in the picture. Each tile is I ft².

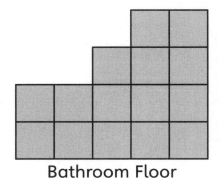

Bathroom Floor

a) What is the area of the bathroom floor?

Area = _____ ft²

b) Yu puts the same size tiles on her kitchen floor. The area of her kitchen floor is 8I ft². How many tiles does she use for both floors?

_____

c) How many more tiles did Yu use for her kitchen than for her bathroom?

_____

A square with sides 1 yard long is called a **square yard**.

You can write square yard as **yd²** for short.

You can measure area in square yards.

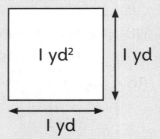

1 yd²   1 yd

1 yd

This is a picture of a square yard.

3. Each grid square is a picture of 1 yd². Find the areas of the shapes.

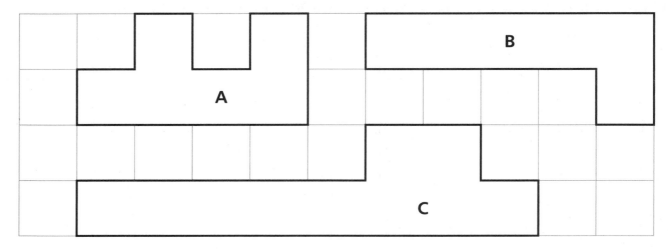

Area of A = _____ yd²   Area of B = _____   Area of C = _____

4. Marco makes a poster using square sheets of paper, as shown in the picture. Each square sheet is 1 yd².

a) What is the area of the poster?

Area = _____

b) Each square sheet of paper costs $4. How much money does Marco spend?

_____

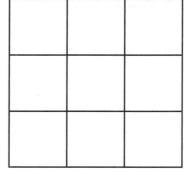

BONUS ▶ Alexa uses 6 of the same square sheets of paper to make a poster. How much money do Alexa and Marco spend altogether?

_____

Measurement and Data 3-31

MD3-32 Finding Area by Skip Counting

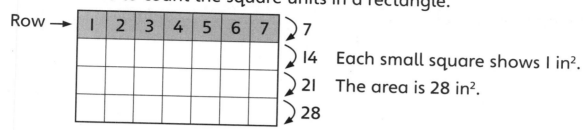

Each small square shows 1 in².

The area is 28 in².

1. Each small square is 1 yd². Use skip counting by rows to find the area.

a)

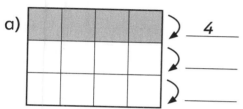

Area = _____ yd²

b)

Area = _____

You can also count the squares in a **column** and skip count columns.

Column

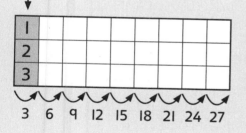

3 square units in each column

9 columns

Area = 27 square units

2. Skip count using the columns to find the area. Each square is 1 ft².

a)

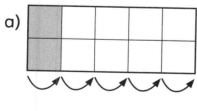

___ ___ ___ ___ ___

Area = _____ ft²

b)

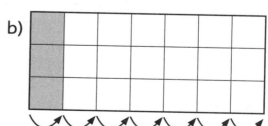

___ ___ ___ ___ ___ ___ ___

Area = _____

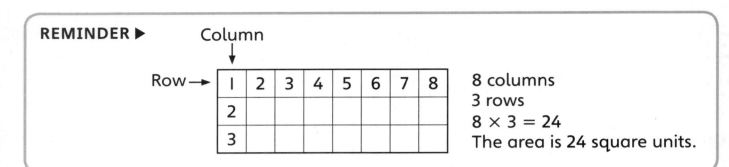

Column
Row →

1	2	3	4	5	6	7	8
2							
3							

8 columns
3 rows
$8 \times 3 = 24$
The area is 24 square units.

3. Count the number of columns and the number of rows. Multiply to find the area. Include the units.

a) 1 square unit = 1 yd²

1	2	3	4	5
2				
3				

___5___ columns

___3___ rows

Area = ___$5 \times 3 = 15$ yd²___

b) 1 square unit = 1 ft²

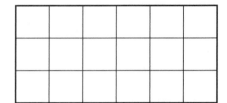

_____ columns

_____ rows

Area = _____

c) 1 square unit = 1 in²

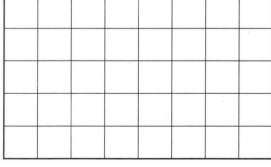

_____ columns

_____ rows

Area = _____

d) 1 square unit = 1 ft²

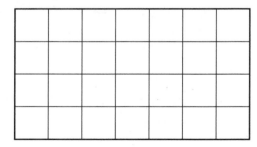

_____ columns

_____ rows

Area = _____

MD3-33 Area of a Rectangle

1. Use a ruler to join the marks and divide the rectangle into square units.
   Use skip counting to find the area of the rectangle.

a)
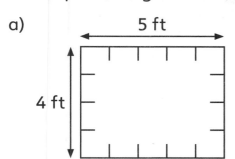

Area = _____ *ft²*

b)
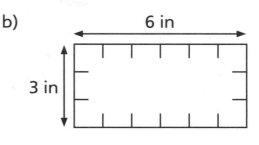

Area = _____

c)
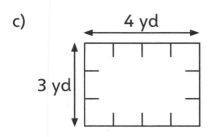

Area = _____

d)
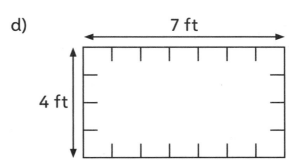

Area = _____

e)
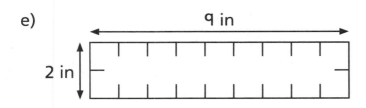

Area = _____

2. For each rectangle in Question 1, multiply the length and width to
   find the area.

   a) Area = __5__ × __4__ = __20 ft²__   b) Area = _____ × _____ = _____

   c) Area = _____ × _____ = _____   d) Area = _____ × _____ = _____

   e) Area = _____ × _____ = _____

3. a) Did you get the same answers in Questions 1 and 2? _____

   b) Explain why the answers should be the same.

4. Fill in the blanks to find the area.

a)

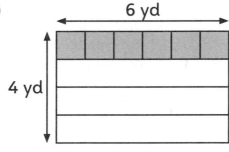

_____ square yards in each row

_____ rows

Area = _____ × _____

= _____ yd²

b)

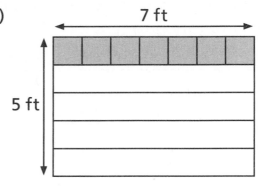

_____ square feet in each row

_____ rows

Area = _____ × _____

= _____

c)

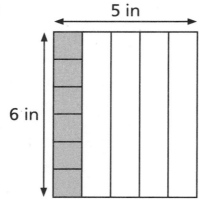

_____ square inches in each column

_____ columns

Area = _____ × _____

= _____ in²

d)

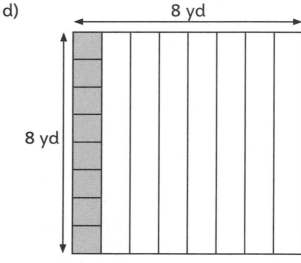

_____ square yards in each column

_____ columns

Area = _____ × _____

= _____

5. Use a ruler to measure the length and width of the rectangle in inches.
Multiply length and width to find the area.

a)　　　　　　　Length = _____ *in*

　　　　　　　　　　　　　　　　　　　　　　　Width = _____ *in*

Area = _____ × _____ = _____ *in²*

b)　　　　　　　　　　　　　　Length = _____ *in*

Width = _____

Area = _____ × _____ = _____

6. Ravi has a small American flag, as shown in the picture.
What is the area of the flag?

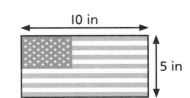

10 in

5 in

7. Tina's lawn is a rectangle 9 yards long and 8 yards wide.
What is the area of Tina's lawn in square yards?

Milly finds the area in two different ways.

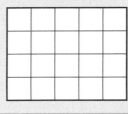

5 columns

4 rows

Method I

$4 \times 5 = 20$

↑
Number of rows

Method 2

$5 \times 4 = 20$

↑
Number of columns

I. Find the area in two different ways.

a)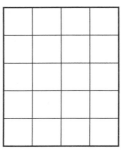

Method I: _____ × _____ = _____

↑
Number of rows

Method 2: _____ × _____ = _____

↑
Number of columns

b)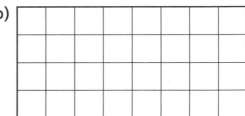

Method I: _____ × _____ = _____

Method 2: _____ × _____ = _____

c)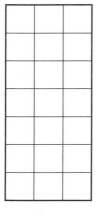

Method I: _____ × _____ = _____

Method 2: _____ × _____ = _____

d)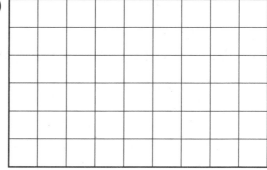

Method I: _____ × _____ = _____

Method 2: _____ × _____ = _____

2. Ivan finds the area of a rectangle by writing the number of rows first. Then he turns the rectangle on its side. Fill in the blanks to find the area.

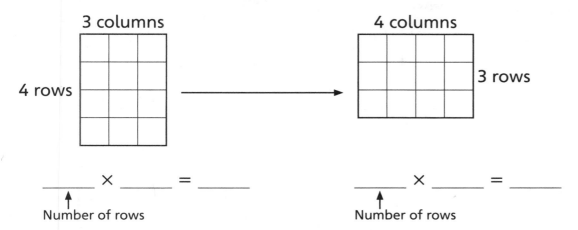

3 columns

4 rows

4 columns

3 rows

_____ × _____ = _____

Number of rows

_____ × _____ = _____

Number of rows

3. Find the area of the garden in two different ways.

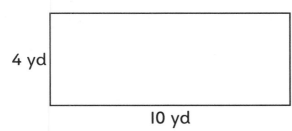

4 yd

10 yd

Area = length × width

= _____ × _____

= _____ yd²

Area = width × length

= _____ × _____

= _____ yd²

4. Josh buys a plastic cover for his swimming pool. The length of the cover is 9 yd and the width is 7 yd.

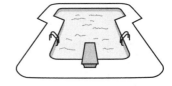

a) Find the area of the cover in two different ways.

Area = _____   Area = _____

b) The price of the cover is $1 per square yard.

How much money does Josh spend? _____

5. Emma finds the area of a rectangle by multiplying length times width. Liz finds the area of the same rectangle by multiplying width times length. Do they get the same answer? Explain.

1. Find the area of each shape in square units.

a) **A.** 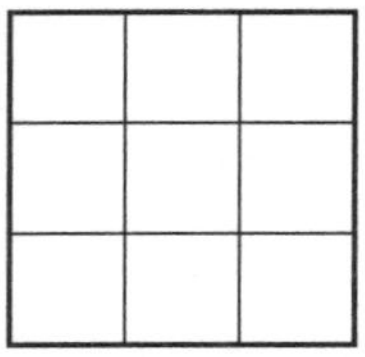 **B.** 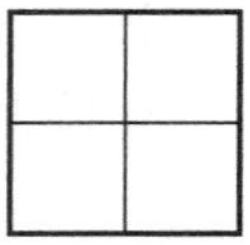 **C.**

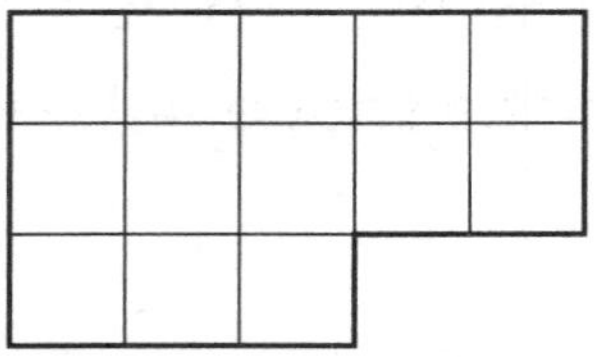

Area of A = _____   Area of B = _____   Area of C = _____

b) **A.** 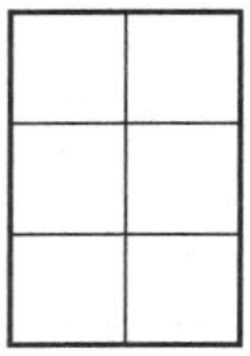 **B.** 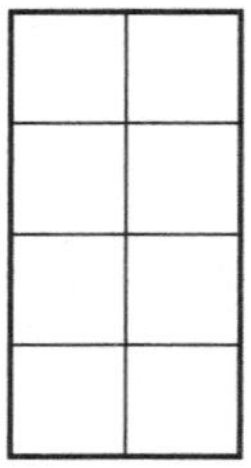 **C.**

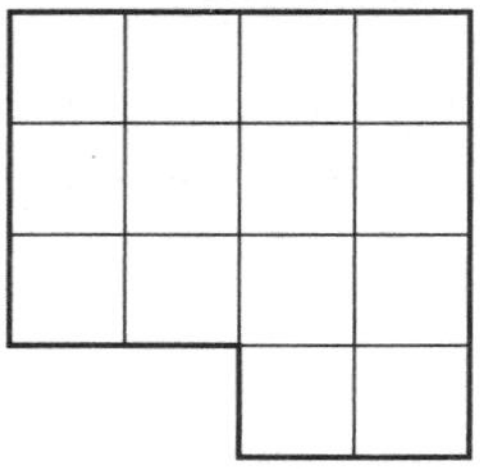

Area of A = _____   Area of B = _____   Area of C = _____

c) **A.** 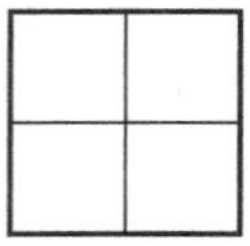 **B.** 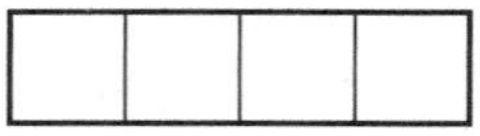 **C.**

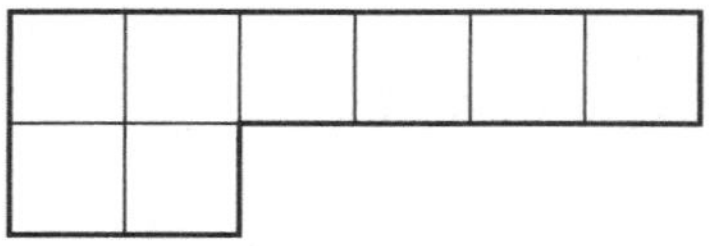

Area of A = _____   Area of B = _____   Area of C = _____

d) **A.** 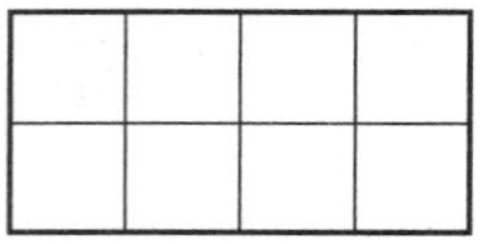 **B.** 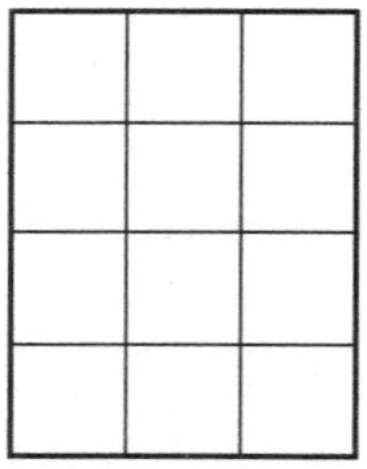 **C.**

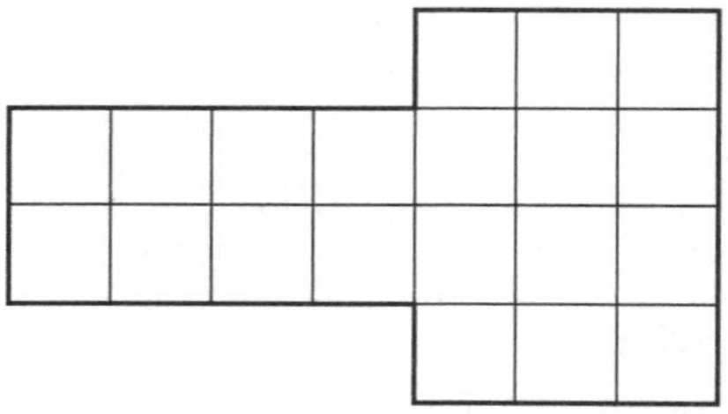

Area of A = _____   Area of B = _____   Area of C = _____

2. Draw a line to show how shape C can be divided into rectangles A and B in each part of Question 1.

3. How can you get the area of shape C from the areas of rectangles A and B in each part of Question 1?

_____

Area of gray rectangle = 3 × 4 = 12 ft²
Area of white rectangle = 2 × 5 = 10 ft²

Area of the shape = 12 + 10 = 22 ft²

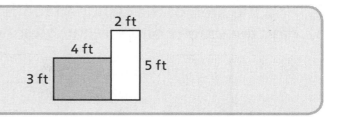

4. Find the areas of the gray and white rectangles. Add the areas of the rectangles to find the area of the shape.

a)

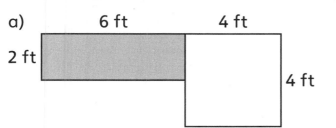

Gray area = _____ × _____

= _____ ft²

White area = _____ × _____

= _____ ft²

Area of shape = _____ + _____

= _____ ft²

b)

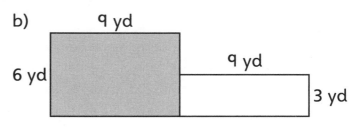

Gray area = _____ × _____

= _____ yd²

White area = _____ × _____

= _____ yd²

Area of shape = _____ + _____

= _____ yd²

c)

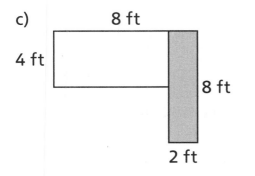

Gray area = _____

White area = _____

Area of shape = _____

d)

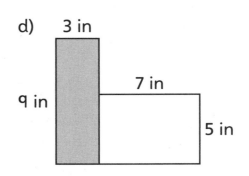

Gray area = _____

White area = _____

Area of shape = _____

5. Find the area of the L-shaped room.
Hint: Shade one of the rectangles. Add the areas of both rectangles.

a)

2 yd

7 yd

5 yd

3 yd

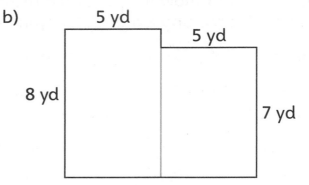

b)

5 yd

5 yd

8 yd

7 yd

Area 1 = _____ yd²

Area 2 = _____ yd²

Total area = _____ yd²

Area 1 = _____

Area 2 = _____

Total area = _____

6. Draw a line to divide the L-shaped garden into two smaller rectangles.
Then find the area of the garden.

a)

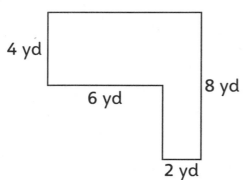

4 yd

6 yd

8 yd

2 yd

b)

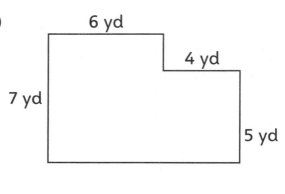

6 yd

4 yd

7 yd

5 yd

Area 1 = _____ yd²

Area 2 = _____ yd²

Total area = _____ yd²

Area 1 = _____

Area 2 = _____

Total area = _____

7. Ed plants flowers in the garden shown in Question 6.b).
He plants 2 flowers in each square yard.
How many flowers does Ed plant in total?

MD3-36 Splitting Rectangles

> Ross wants to show 5 × 4 using a rectangle.
> He draws a rectangle 5 units long and 4 units wide.
>
> The area of the rectangle is 20 square units.
>
> The product of 5 and 4 is 20.
>
> 5 × 4 = 20

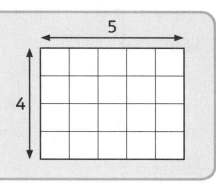

1. Draw a rectangle on the grid to show the multiplication. Find the product.

   a) 5 × 6 = _____   b) 7 × 4 = _____

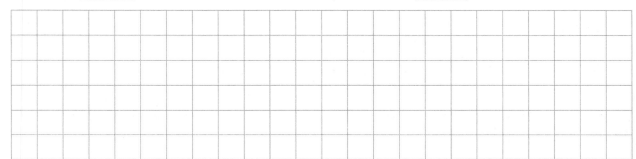

2. Find the area of the gray rectangle and the area of the white rectangle. Add the areas.

   a)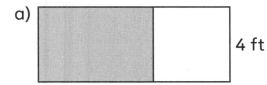

   4 ft

   6 ft   4 ft

   Gray area = _____ × _____

   = _____ ft²

   White area = _____ × _____

   = _____ ft²

   Total area = _____ + _____

   = _____ ft²

   b)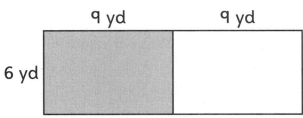

   9 yd   9 yd

   6 yd

   Gray area = _____ × _____

   = _____

   White area = _____ × _____

   = _____

   Total area = _____ + _____

   = _____

You can find the area of a large rectangle in two different ways.

Method 1

Gray area = 8 × 5 = 40 yd²

White area = 8 × 2 = 16 yd²

Add the areas: 40 + 16 = ⑤⑥ yd²

Method 2

Add the widths: 5 + 2 = 7 yd

Length = 8 yd

Multiply: 8 × 7 = ⑤⑥ yd²

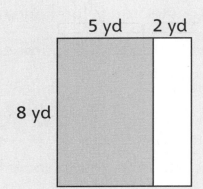

3. Find the area of the large rectangle in two different ways.

a)

Gray area = _____ × _____ = _____ in²

White area = _____ × _____ = _____ in²

Total area = _____ + _____ = _____ in²

Length of large rectangle = _____ + _____ = _____ in

Width of large rectangle = _____ in

Area of large rectangle = _____ × _____ = _____ in²

b)

Gray area = _____ × _____ = _____ ft²

White area = _____ × _____ = _____ ft²

Total area = _____ + _____ = _____ ft²

Length of large rectangle = _____ ft

Width of large rectangle = _____ + _____ = _____ ft

Area of large rectangle = _____ × _____ = _____ ft²

4. Kim wants to multiply 8 and 16. She draws the picture below. Complete Kim's work.

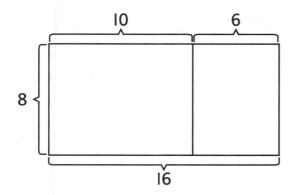

$8 \times 16 = (8 \times 10) + (8 \times 6)$

$= \underline{\hspace{1cm}} + \underline{\hspace{1cm}}$

$= \underline{\hspace{1cm}}$

5. Fill in the blanks to find the product.

a)

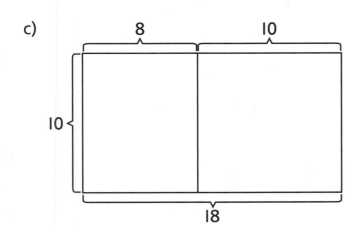

$4 \times 8 = (4 \times \underline{\ 5\ }) + (4 \times \underline{\hspace{1cm}})$

$= \underline{\hspace{1cm}} + \underline{\hspace{1cm}}$

$= \underline{\hspace{1cm}}$

b)

$9 \times 17 = (9 \times \underline{\hspace{1cm}}) + (9 \times \underline{\hspace{1cm}})$

$= \underline{\hspace{1cm}} + \underline{\hspace{1cm}}$

$= \underline{\hspace{1cm}}$

c)

$10 \times 18 = (10 \times \underline{\hspace{1cm}}) + (10 \times \underline{\hspace{1cm}})$

$= \underline{\hspace{1cm}} + \underline{\hspace{1cm}}$

$= \underline{\hspace{1cm}}$

MD3-37 Area and Perimeter (I)

> **REMINDER ▶** Perimeter is the distance around a shape.
> Area is the number of square units that cover a shape.

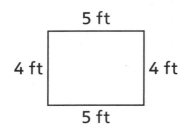

5 ft

4 ft   4 ft

5 ft

Perimeter = 4 + 5 + 4 + 5 = 18 ft

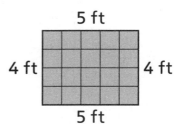

5 ft

4 ft   4 ft

5 ft

Area = 4 × 5 = 20 ft²

I. Fill in the blanks. Then find the perimeter or the area.

a)

7 in

3 in   _3_ in

_7_ in

Perimeter = 3 + 7 + _____ + _____

= _____ in

b)

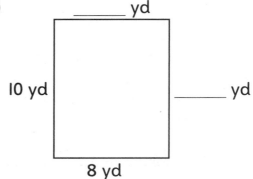

_____ yd

10 yd   _____ yd

8 yd

Area = _____ × _____

= _____ yd²

c)

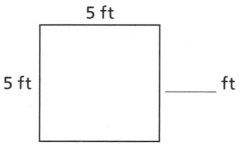

5 ft

5 ft   _____ ft

_____ ft

Perimeter = _____

= _____ ft

d)

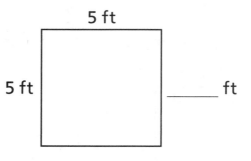

5 ft

5 ft   _____ ft

_____ ft

Area = _____

= _____ ft²

Measurement and Data 3-37

Order does not matter in addition. You can add the long sides first.

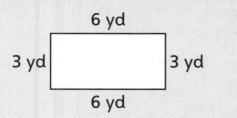

6 yd

3 yd   3 yd

6 yd

Perimeter = (6 + 6) + (3 + 3)

= (2 × 6) + (2 × 3)

= 12 + 6

= 18 yd

2. Fill in the blanks to find the perimeter.

a)

7 yd

4 yd   4 yd

7 yd

Perimeter = (2 × _____) + (2 × _____)

= _____ + _____ = _____ yd

b)

8 ft

6 ft   6 ft

8 ft

Perimeter = (2 × _____) + (2 × _____)

= _____ + _____ = _____

Beth learns an easy way to find the perimeter of a square.

3 in

3 in   3 in

3 in

Perimeter = 3 + 3 + 3 + 3

= 3 × 4

= 12 in

Beth multiplies the length of one side by 4.

3. Find the perimeter and the area of the square. Include the units.

a)

7 ft

7 ft

_____

_____

Perimeter = 4 × _____ = _____

Area = _____ × _____ = _____

b)

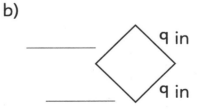

_____   9 in

_____   9 in

Perimeter = 4 × _____ = _____

Area = _____ × _____ = _____

MD3-38 Missing Sides in a Rectangle

> The perimeter of a rectangle is 10 ft. Each side measurement is a whole number. What is the length and width?
>
> Let's try different widths. Try 1 ft first.
>
> The widths add to 2 ft.
>
> The missing lengths are 10 − 2 = 8 ft altogether.
>
> Each length is 8 ÷ 2 = 4 ft.

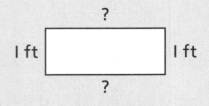

1. Find the missing length of the rectangle.

   The widths add to _____ ft.

   The missing lengths are

   _____ − _____ = _____ ft altogether.

   Each length is _____ ÷ 2 = _____ ft.

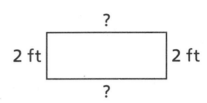

Perimeter = 10 ft

> The area of a rectangle is 36 ft².
>
> The length is 9 ft. Find the width.
>
> 36 ÷ 9 = 4 ft.
>
> The width is 4 ft.

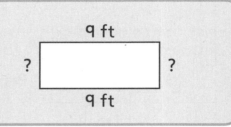

2. The area of a rectangle is 35 ft². The length is 7 ft. Find the width.

   _____ ÷ _____ = _____   The width is _____.

3. The playground in a school has the shape of a rectangle and is 10 yd long. The area of the playground is 80 yd². How wide is the playground?

4. Mike's window is a rectangle with an area of 54 ft². The window measures 9 ft across. How tall is the window?

BONUS ▶ A field in a park has the shape of a square. The area is 25 yd². What is the length of each side of the field?

I. a) Fill in the blanks. Then find the perimeter and area of each
    rectangle. Write the answers in the table below.

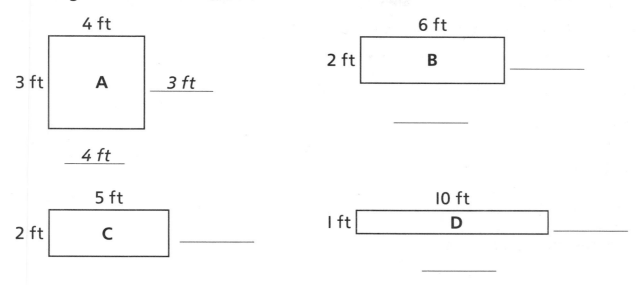

4 ft

3 ft   A   _3 ft_

_4 ft_

6 ft

2 ft   B   _____

_____

5 ft

2 ft   C   _____

_____

10 ft

1 ft   D   _____

_____

Rectangle	Perimeter	Area
A	3 + 4 + 3 + 4 = 14 ft	3 × 4 = 12 ft²
B		
C		
D		

b) Which rectangle has the same area as rectangle A? _____

Do these two rectangles have the same perimeter? _____

c) Which rectangle has the same area as rectangle C? _____

Do these two rectangles have the same perimeter? _____

d) Which rectangle has a larger perimeter, A or D? _____

Which rectangle has a larger area, A or D? _____

e) Which rectangle has the same perimeter as rectangle A? _____

Do these two rectangles have the same area? _____

The rectangles below have the same perimeter, but different areas.

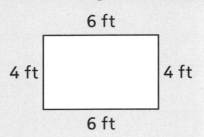

6 ft

4 ft   4 ft

6 ft

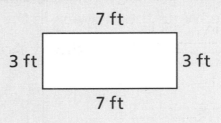

7 ft

3 ft   3 ft

7 ft

Perimeter = 4 + 6 + 4 + 6 = 20 ft

Area = 4 × 6 = 24 ft²

Perimeter = 3 + 7 + 3 + 7 = 20 ft

Area = 3 × 7 = 21 ft²

2. Draw two rectangles on the grid so that the areas are different but the perimeter for each rectangle is 14 units. Write the areas below.

Area = _____   Area = _____

3. Draw two rectangles on the grid so that the areas are different but the perimeter for each rectangle is 24 units. Write the areas below.

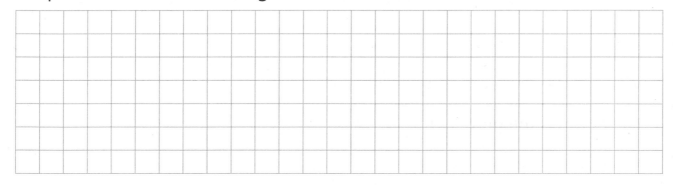

Area = _____   Area = _____

BONUS ▶ On a grid, draw rectangles so that the area of each rectangle is 36 square units. Draw as many different rectangles as you can. Write their perimeters.

MD3-40 Puzzles and Problems

I. Find the area of the large rectangle in two different ways.

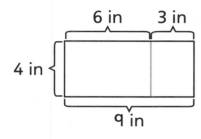

Method I: Area = 4 × 9 = _____ in²

Method 2: Area = (4 × _____) + (4 × _____)

$\qquad$ = _____ + _____

$\qquad$ = _____ in²

2. Find the area of the L-shaped garden.

a)

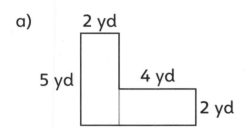

Area I = _____ yd²

Area 2 = _____ yd²

Total area = _____ yd²

b)

Area I = _____

Area 2 = _____

Total area = _____

3. Eddy's garden is a rectangle 5 yards wide and 8 yards long.

a) What is the area of the garden? _____

b) Eddy divides the garden into four parts of the same size.

What is the area of each part? _____

c) Rani's garden is a rectangle 7 yards wide and 9 yards long.

What is the area of Rani's garden? _____

d) How much larger is Rani's garden than Eddy's? _____

4. Blanca and Greg are painting walls.

a) Blanca's wall is a rectangle 9 ft long.
The area of the wall is 63 ft².
What is the height of the wall?

b) Greg's wall is 8 ft long and 8 ft high.
What is the area of the wall?

c) Blanca and Greg have a can of paint
that can cover an area of 120 ft².
Do they have enough paint for both walls?

5. Jon wants to put tiles on his bathroom floor. The width of the floor
is 7 ft and the area is 56 ft².

a) What is the length of the bathroom floor?

b) What is the perimeter of the bathroom floor?

c) Each tile is 1 square foot. How many tiles will Jon need?

d) Each tile costs $3. How much money will Jon spend?

6. Anna needs to mow an L-shaped lawn, as shown
in the picture.

a) What is the area of the lawn?

b) Anna gets paid $2 for each square meter of the lawn
that she mows. How much money does she earn?

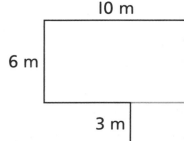

7. Eva makes a paper rectangle 3 inches wide and 7 inches long.
Zack makes a paper rectangle 4 inches wide and 6 inches long.

a) How much more paper did Zack use than Eva?

b) How much paper did Zack and Eva use altogether?

BONUS ▸ Does 5 × 8 = (5 × 6) + (5 × 2)?
Explain using the picture.

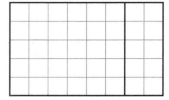

MD3-41 Liquid Volume

1. Circle the bottle with more liquid.

a)    b)    c)

2. Circle the glass with less liquid.

a)    b)    c)

3. Circle the container with more liquid.

a)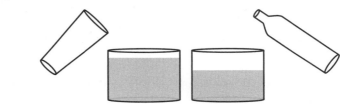

b)

c)

BONUS ▶ Circle the container with the most liquid.

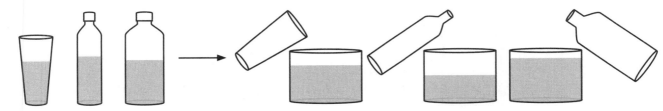

4. Circle the container that holds more.

a)

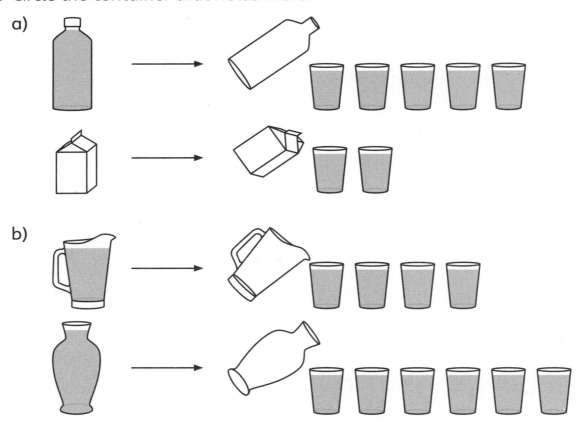

b)

5. Circle the container that holds less.

a)

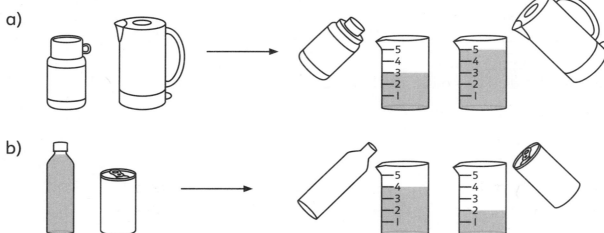

b)

BONUS ▶ Circle the container that holds more.

MD3-42 Liters and Milliliters

The **capacity** of a container is how much it can hold.

1. Circle the container with greater capacity.

a)

b)

c)

d)

Capacity can be measured in **liters (L)**.

A quart of milk and $\frac{1}{4}$ of a cup together make up about a liter.

2. Circle the containers that have a capacity of about 1 L each.

The **volume** of a liquid is how much space it takes up.

The container has a capacity of 3 L.

The water in the container has a volume of 2 L.

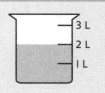

3. Find the capacity of the container and the volume of the liquid.

a)

Capacity = _____ L

Volume = _____ L

b)

Capacity = _____ L

Volume = _____ L

c)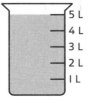

Capacity = _____ L

Volume = _____ L

Smaller volumes are often measured in **milliliters (mL)**.

There are 1,000 milliliters in a liter.

There are about 5 mL in a teaspoon.

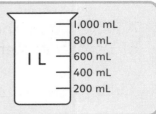

4. Circle the containers that have a capacity of less than 1 L each.

5. Find the capacity of the container and the volume of the liquid.

a)

Capacity = _____ mL

Volume = _____ mL

b)

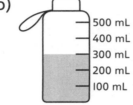

Capacity = _____ mL

Volume = _____ mL

c)

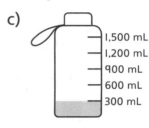

Capacity = _____ mL

Volume = _____ mL

6. Nancy fills a measuring cup with 40 mL of water. She pours out some water and has 30 mL left in the cup. How much water did she pour out?

_____

_____

7. Estimate the capacity in milliliters. Then use a measuring cup to measure the capacity.

a) a glass   b) a bowl   c) a water bottle

8. Estimate the capacity in liters. Then use a liter bottle to measure the capacity.

a) a sink   b) a bucket   c) a large jug

      Measurement and Data 3-42

1. A water cooler has a capacity of 20 L. What is the total capacity of 3 water coolers?

   60L. at a time

2. A cook pours 75 mL of water and 15 mL of milk into a bowl. What is the total volume of the liquids in the bowl?

   90 that is thick and good

3. Amy has to take 10 mL of medicine 2 times a day.

   a) How much will she take in 1 day?

   uh, 20.

   b) How much will she take over 4 days?

   80. I not num

4. The capacity of a bottle of apple juice is approximately 300 mL. Find the total capacity in milliliters of 3 bottles of juice.

   900 so next page

5. A car uses 6 L of gasoline each day.

   6L

   a) How much gasoline does it use in one week?

   6×7=42

   b) The car's gas tank has a capacity of 40 L. Will the driver have to fill the tank before the end of the week? Explain.

   yes

6. Jug A has a capacity of 5 L. Jug B has a capacity of 3 L. Peter fills Jug A with water to its capacity. He then pours water from Jug A into Jug B until Jug B is full, as shown in the picture. What is the volume of water left in Jug A?

Jug A   Jug B

2L   5-2=3

7. The capacities of three tubs are shown in the picture. Bev fills Tub A and Tub B with water, then empties both into Tub C.

A 30 L   B 20 L   C 120 L

   a) What is the total volume of water in Tub C?

50 yay...

   b) What volume of water must be added to Tub C to fill it to its capacity?

>0L

8. A water tank that has 180 L of water in it starts leaking. It loses 30 L of water each day.

WATER TANK

   a) How much water is left after 2 days?

120   60
          20 ⟌ 180

   b) How much water is left after 4 days?

60   60
       30 ⟌ 180

   BONUS ▶ How many days will it take for the water tank to empty?

6 Days

> **Mass** is the amount of matter in an object.
>
> The heavier the object, the greater the mass.

1. Circle the object with more mass.

a)

b)

c)

2. Circle the object with less mass.

a)

b)

c)

> A **balance** is used to find if two objects have the same mass.
>
> equal   heavier   lighter
>
>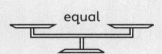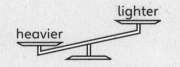

3. Circle the heavier object.

a)

b)

c)

d)

e)

f)

4. Circle the lighter object.

a)   b)   c)

5. Circle the heavier object. Check the balance beside the objects.

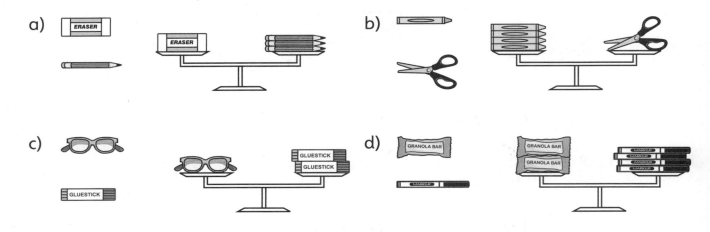

a)   b)

c)   d)

6. Circle the heavier object. Check the balances beside the objects.

a)

b)

BONUS ▶ Circle the heaviest object.

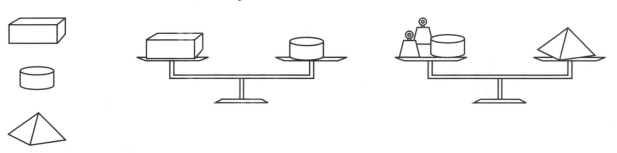

MD3-45 Grams and Kilograms

The mass of small objects can be measured in **grams**.
You write **1 g** for 1 gram. A large paper clip weighs about 1 g.
A nickel weighs 5 g. You can measure mass with a **scale**.

 1 g   5 g

1. Circle the objects that have a mass of about 1 g each.

The mass of larger objects can be measured in **kilograms**.
You write **1 kg** for 1 kilogram. A liter of water has a mass of 1 kg.
There are 1,000 g in 1 kilogram.

 1 kg

2. Circle the objects that have a mass of about 1 kg each.

3. Estimate the mass of the object in grams. Then use a scale to measure the mass.

a) a 25¢ coin

Estimate: _____

Mass: _____

b) a notebook

Estimate: _____

Mass: _____

c) a calculator

Estimate: _____

Mass: _____

d) a pen

Estimate: _____

Mass: _____

e) a cell phone

Estimate: _____

Mass: _____

f) scissors

Estimate: _____

Mass: _____

4. Estimate the mass of the object in kilograms. Then use a scale to measure the mass.

a) a stack of books

b) a backpack

c) a student

d) a laptop

e) a desk

f) an adult

5. Circle which unit is better for measuring the mass of the object.

a)

g   kg

b)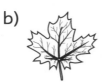

g   kg

c)

g   kg

d)

g   kg

6. Write the missing mass needed to make the balance level.

a)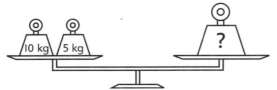

? = _____

b)

? = _____

7. Circle the better estimate for the mass of the object.

a)

100 g   100 kg

b)

800 g   800 kg

c)

10 g   10 kg

d)

5,000 g   5,000 kg

8. Circle the better estimate for the mass of the object.

a) a pen cap   1 g   1 kg

b) two loaves of bread   1 g   1 kg

c) a laptop   1 g   1 kg

d) a dollar bill   1 g   1 kg

BONUS ▶ 1 kilogram is 1,000 grams. Write the mass in grams.

a) 2 kg   b) 3 kg   c) 5 kg   d) 10 kg

_____ g   _____ g   _____ g   _____ g

MD3-46 Mass Word Problems

1. Mandy's granola bar has 3 g of protein.
   How much protein is in 6 granola bars?

   _____

   _____

2. Bob piles boxes with masses of 54 kg, 32 kg, 26 kg, and 75 kg on a cart.

   a) What is the total mass of the boxes?

   b) The cart can carry a maximum of 200 kg. What is the greatest mass
      of a box that Bob can add to the cart?

3. A bag of cement has a mass of 25 kg. Find the total mass of 4 bags
   of cement.

   _____

   _____

4. There are 5 identical boxes in a delivery truck.
   The total mass of the boxes is 35 kg.
   What is the mass of each box?

   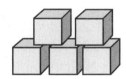

   _____

   _____

5. Jen says that her dog has a mass of about 10 L. Is this correct? Explain.

   _____

   _____

6. A nickel has a mass of 5 g.

   a) What is the mass of 4 nickels?

   b) What is the mass of 10 nickels?

   BONUS ▶ What is the mass of 100 nickels?

7. The mass of 30 grains of rice is about 6 g.

   a) About how many grains are in 1 g of rice?

   b) About how many grains are in 8 g of rice?

   BONUS ▶ About how many grains are in 100 g of rice?

8. The mass of 200 ants is 1 g.

   a) How many ants have a mass of 2 g altogether?

   b) How many ants have a mass of 3 g altogether?

   BONUS ▶ What is the mass of 800 ants?

9. The barbell holds two 20 kg weights and two 10 kg weights. The barbell itself has a mass of 10 kg. What is the total mass of the barbell and the weights?

_____

_____

10. John has a mass of 28 kg. Sun has a mass of 23 kg. Mike has a mass of 27 kg. What mass should Yu have so that the friends balance?

11. Fly Me Airlines allows a passenger to bring luggage for free up to a limit of 23 kg. It charges a fee of $20 for each kilogram over 23 kg. Bo's luggage has a mass of 27 kg.

   a) How much over the limit is Bo's luggage?

_____

_____

   b) How much extra does Bo have to pay?

_____

_____

A **picture graph** uses **symbols** to show **data**.

On this picture graph, the symbol ♀ means I student.

2 students eat lunch at home.

5 students eat lunch at school.

Lunch Location

At home	♀ ♀
At school	♀ ♀ ♀ ♀ ♀

I. Use the picture graph to answer the question.

Number of Rainy Days

April	⬤	⬤	⬤	⬤	⬤	⬤	⬤	⬤
May	⬤	⬤	⬤	⬤	⬤			
June	⬤	⬤	⬤	⬤				
July	⬤	⬤	⬤					
August	⬤	⬤	⬤	⬤				
September								

⬤ = I day

a) How many rainy days were there in each month?

June _____   May _____   August _____

b) Which month had only 3 rainy days? _____

c) Which months had the same number of rainy days? _____

d) How many more rainy days were there in April than in August? _____

e) June has 30 days. How many days were not rainy?

Write the subtraction equation. _____

f) September had 7 rainy days. Show this on the picture graph.

g) Which month had the most rainy days? _____

h) Which month had the fewest rainy days? _____

2. Use the picture graph to answer the questions.

a) **Lunch for Jim's Class**   😊 = I student

| At school | 😊 😊 😊 😊 😊 😊 😊 |
| At home | 😊 😊 😊 😊 😊 😊 😊 😊 😊 😊 😊 |

Do more students from Jim's class eat lunch at home or

at school? _____ How many more? _____

b) **Lunch for Kate's Class**   😊 = I student

| At school | 😊 😊   😊   😊 😊   😊 😊 😊 |
| At home | 😊 😊 😊 😊 😊   😊 😊 😊 😊 |

Kate thinks more students eat lunch at school. Is she correct? _____

c) Fix the picture graph in part b) so that it is easier to read.

Lunch for Kate's Class   😊 = I student

| At school | | | | | | | | | | | |
| At home | | | | | | | | | | | |

Do more students from Kate's class eat lunch at home or

at school? _____ How many more? _____

d) Use the data from the picture graphs in parts a) and c) to make a new graph.

Lunch at School   😊 = I student

| Jim's class | | | | | | | | | | | |
| Kate's class | | | | | | | | | | | |

Do more students from Jim's class or Kate's class

eat at school? _____ How many more? _____

3. Ross asked his friends to vote for their favorite sport.

   a) Draw a circle for each student vote.

Favorite Sport	Number of Students
Baseball	5
Football	6
Ice Hockey	3
Soccer	4

Student's Favorite Sports   ◯ = 1 student

Baseball	◯	◯	◯	◯	◯	
Football						
Ice Hockey						
Soccer						

   b) Which sport is the most popular? _____

   How can you see that from the picture graph? _____

   _____

   c) How many more students voted for baseball than ice hockey? _____

   d) How many students in total voted for ball games? _____

   BONUS ▶ How many more students voted for ball games than

   for ice hockey? _____

4. Some students from Jane's class go to after-school programs.

   a) Draw circles to show the data.

   6 students go to art lessons.

   3 more students go to soccer than to art lessons.

   2 fewer students go to music lessons than to art lessons.

   After-School Programs   ◯ = 1 student

Art										
Soccer										
Music										
No program										

   b) There are 23 students in Jane's class. How many do not go to any after-school programs? Show this on the picture graph.

MD3-48 Picture Graphs

A **scale** shows what the symbol means on a picture graph.

10 students eat lunch at home and 20 students eat lunch at school. Both picture graphs show the same data but they use different scales.

Lunch Location

At home	☺
At school	☺ ☺

Lunch Location

At home	☺ ☺
At school	☺ ☺ ☺ ☺

☺ = 10 students ⟵ ── scale ── ⟶ ☺ = 5 students

1. Look at the scale and multiply to find what each group of symbols means.

   a) ☺ = 5 people

   ☺☺☺ = __15__ people   ☺☺☺☺☺ = _____ people

   b) ✿ = 2 flowers

   ✿ ✿ = _____ flowers   ✿ ✿ ✿ ✿ = _____ flowers

   ✿ ✿ ✿ ✿ ✿ ✿ ✿ = _____ flowers

   c) ☐ = 3 boxes

   ☐☐☐ = _____ boxes   ☐☐☐☐☐ = _____ boxes

   ☐☐☐☐☐☐ = _____ boxes   ☐☐☐☐☐☐☐☐☐ = _____ boxes

BONUS ▶ If 😊 = 20 people, how many people is 😊 😊 😊 😊 😊 ? _____

2. Look at the scale and draw symbols to show each number.

   a) ☐ = 4 boxes

   12 boxes = ☐☐☐   8 boxes =

   b) ☐ = 5 boxes

   15 boxes =   30 boxes =

3. a) Use the picture graph to fill in the table.

Flowers in Pedro's Garden   🌷 = 2 flowers

Flowers in Pedro's Garden	
Roses	🌷 🌷 🌷 🌷
Pansies	🌷 🌷
Marigolds	🌷 🌷 🌷 🌷 🌷 🌷

Type of Flower	Number of Flowers
Roses	
Pansies	
Marigolds	

b) Use the data in part a) to draw a picture graph with the new scale.

Flowers in Pedro's Garden   🌷 = 4 flowers

Flowers in Pedro's Garden					
Roses					
Pansies					
Marigolds					

c) How many more marigolds than pansies does Pedro have? _____

d) How many flowers does Pedro have in total? _____

> Half a symbol means half the number. Example: If ☺ = 4, then (= 4 ÷ 2 = 2.

4. The first row shows what ☺ means. What does (mean? Fill in the table.

☺	10	2	6	20	14	12	200
(	5						

> If ☺ = 10, then ☺ ☺ ☺ = 3 × 10 = 30, and ☺ ☺ ☺ (= 30 + 5 = 35.

5. The first row shows what one symbol means. What does each group of symbols mean?

a)

☆	6	2	10
☆☆	12		
⛢	3		
☆☆⛢	15		

b)

⚥	2	4	10
⚥⚥⚥⚥			
⚧			
⚥⚥⚥⚥⚧			

I. a) There are 25 shapes in the picture.
Count the number of each shape.

Shape	Number of Shapes
Triangle	
Quadrilateral	
Pentagon	
Hexagon	
Circle	

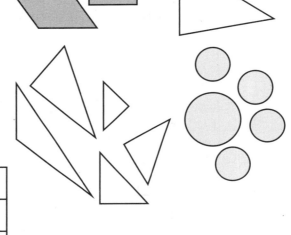

b) Choose a symbol for your picture graph. Make sure it is easy to draw half a symbol.

_____

c) Draw a picture graph using your symbol. Remember to fill in the scale.

Shapes in the Picture

Triangle						
Quadrilateral						
Pentagon						
Hexagon						
Circle						

_____ = 2 shapes

d) What is the most common shape in the picture? _____

What is the least common shape in the picture? _____

e) Polygons have straight sides.
How many polygons are in the picture? _____

f) How many more polygons than circles are in the picture? _____

2. The first line shows the data. Circle the best scale for the data.

a) 12, 6, 8

(☆ = 2)

☆ = 5

☆ = 10

b) 30, 20, 40

☆ = 2

☆ = 3

☆ = 10

c) 9, 12, 6

☆ = 3

☆ = 5

☆ = 10

d) 25, 10, 35

☆ = 2

☆ = 3

☆ = 5

3. Lily counted the students in each grade at camp.

Grade	K	1	2	3	4	5
Number of Students	15	20	30	20	30	25

Draw a picture graph with the given scale.

a) ☺ = 5 students

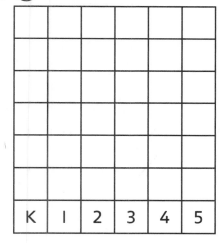

b) ☺ = 10 students

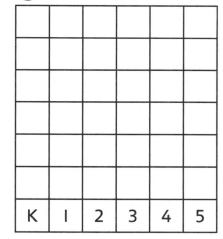

4. Use the picture graph to answer the question.

a) How many more students visited New York than Florida?

b) The number of students who visited Alaska was less than the number for Florida. How many less?

c) 15 more students visited California than Washington. Show this on the picture graph.

States Visited by Students

Alaska	☺
California	☺ ☺ ☺ ☺
Florida	☺ ☺ ☺
New York	☺ ☺ ☺ ☺
Washington	

☺ = 10 students

MD3-50 Introduction to Bar Graphs

A **bar graph** uses **bars** to show data.

Each bar graph has a **title, labels,** two **axes,** and a **scale.**

This bar graph shows that there are 5 cats and 3 dogs in a shelter.

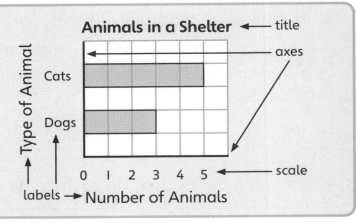

1. The bar graph shows fish at the zoo.

   a) Use the bar graph to fill in the table.

Type of Fish	Number of Fish
Bass	3
Catfish	
Perch	
Sunfish	

   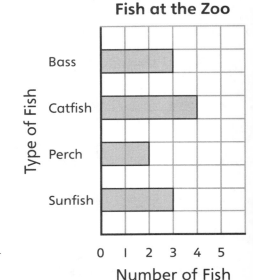

   b) What is the most common fish? _____

   c) What is the least common fish? _____

   d) How many fish are in the zoo in total? _____

2. Use the bar graph to answer the questions.

   a) How many students have black hair? _____

   b) How many students have blond hair? _____

   c) 2 students have red hair. Draw a bar for them.

   d) How many students do not have

      black hair? _____

   e) How many students are in the class? _____

   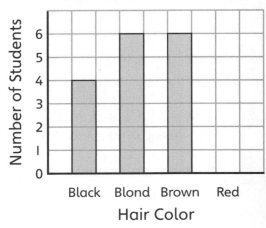

3. Carlos counted birds he saw in the park.

a) Use the table to complete the bar graph.

Birds Seen in the Park

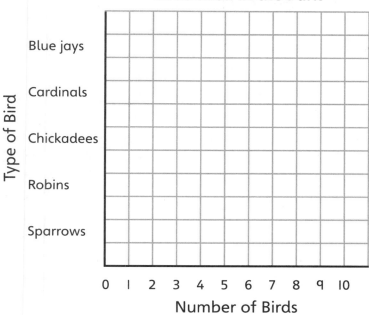

Type of Bird	Number of Birds
Blue jays	2
Cardinals	4
Chickadees	7
Robins	4
Sparrows	10

b) What was the most common bird seen in the park? _____

How does the bar graph show it? _____

c) How many more sparrows than robins did Carlos see? _____

d) How many birds did Carlos see in total? _____

e) A blue jay weighs about 85 g. How much did the blue jays that

Carlos saw weigh altogether? _____

f) A sparrow weighs about 20 g. What weighs more, all the sparrows that Carlos saw or all the blue jays he saw?

g) A chickadee weighs about 10 g. Do all the chickadees Carlos saw weigh more altogether than one blue jay?

h) A cardinal weighs about 45 g. Use doubling to find the weight of all the cardinals Carlos saw.

i) A robin weighs about 80 g. How much do all the robins that Carlos saw weigh altogether?

BONUS ▶ What was the total weight of all the birds Carlos saw?

MD3-51 Bar Graphs

Some bar graphs use skip counting in a scale.

1. Tessa asked her friends which juice they like best. She made a bar graph to show the results.

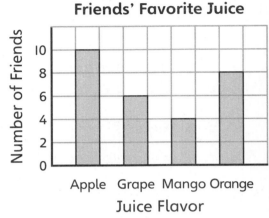

Friends' Favorite Juice

a) What was the most popular flavor?

_____

b) What was the least popular flavor?

_____

c) Roy wants to bring the 2 most popular flavors of juice to a party. Which flavors of juice should he bring?

_____

d) What number does the scale skip count by? _____

e) Skip count to fill in the table using the bar graph.

Juice Flavor	Apple	Grape	Mango	Orange
Number of Friends	10			

2. Rick asked who liked traveling by car, plane, or train the most. He shows the answers in a bar graph.

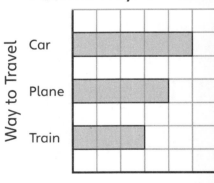

Favorite Ways to Travel

a) What number does the scale

skip count by? _____

b) The bar for car travel is _____ blocks long.

Each block shows _____ students.

c) Use the bar graph to fill in the table.

Way to Travel	Number of Blocks	Multiplication	Number of Students
Car	5	5 × 3 = 15	15
Plane			
Train			

3. A national park asked 100 people to vote for their favorite activity in the park. Some results are shown in the table.

Activity	Number of People
Boating	10
Cycling	
Hiking	15
Swimming	50

a) How many people did not choose cycling?

_____

b) How many people chose cycling? Write this number in the table.

c) What number does the scale in the bar graph in part e) below count by? _____

d) Fill in the table.

Activity	Number of People	Division	Length of Bar (Blocks)
Boating	10	10 ÷ 5 = 2	2
Cycling			
Hiking			
Swimming			

e) Finish the bar graph.

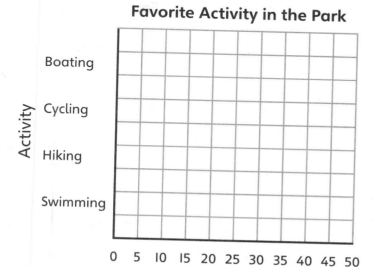

Favorite Activity in the Park

4. Grade 3 students collected coats for charity.

They collected 3 times as many coats in January as in December.

They collected 6 more coats in February than in December.

Altogether, they collected 18 coats.

a) Use the clues above to fill in the missing bars.

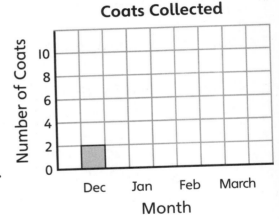

Coats Collected

b) In which month did students collect the

most coats? _____

c) In which two months did students collect the same

number of coats? _____ and _____

d) How many fewer coats did students collect in March

than in February? _____

5. The bar graph shows how much snow fell in Minneapolis, MN, during the year.

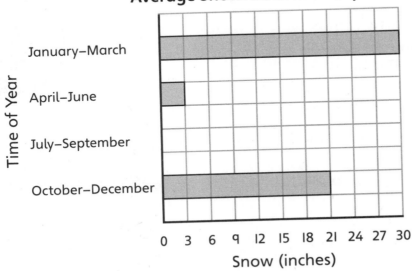

Average Snowfall in Minneapolis, MN

a) How many more inches of snow fell in the first three months of the year than in the last three months of the year?

b) How much snow fell in the whole year?

c) Which months have no bar? Explain why this makes sense.

MD3-52 Scales on Bar Graphs

A bar can end between two numbers on a bar graph.

1. Students voted for their favorite summer activity. The bar graph shows the results.

   a) Fill in the table.

Favorite Activity	Number of Students
Baseball	5
Soccer	
Swimming	
Windsurfing	

   Favorite Summer Activity

   b) 7 students picked boating. Add the bar for them to the bar graph.

   c) Fill in the blanks.

   _____ fewer students picked soccer than swimming.

   _____ more students picked swimming than baseball.

   _____ students picked water activities.

   _____ more students chose water activities than ball games.

   _____ was the most popular activity.

   _____ was the least popular activity.

   BONUS ▶ Kevin thinks that the bar for swimming is 2 blocks longer than the bar for soccer, so 2 more people voted for swimming. Is he correct? Explain.

   _____

   _____

   _____

2. Jake and Hanna asked their classmates about pets. The bar graphs show the results.

Jake's bar graph:

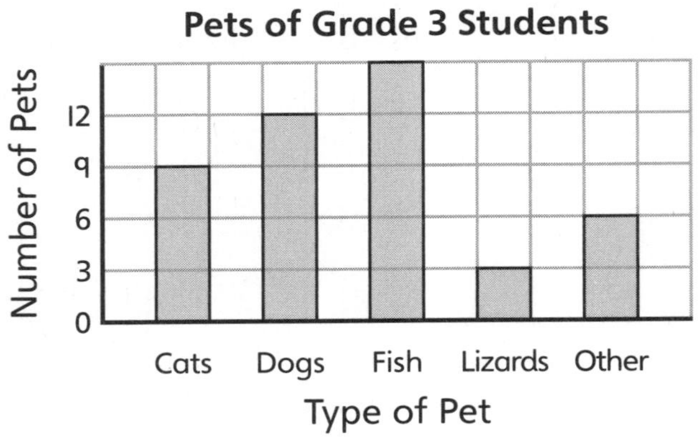

Pets of Grade 3 Students

Hana's bar graph:

Pets of Grade 3 Students

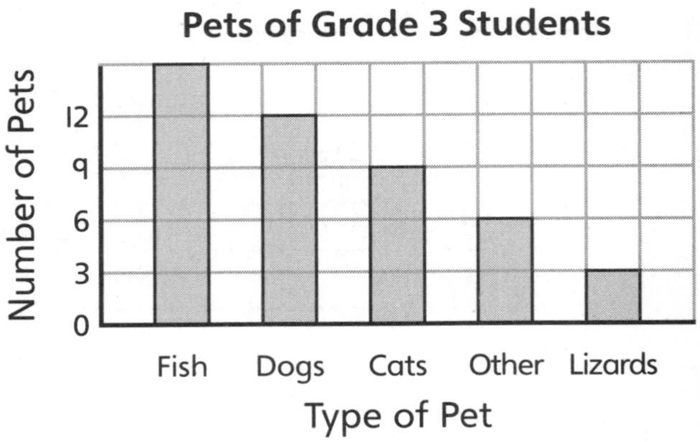

a) Fill in the table.

Pets	Number of Pets	
	Jake's Graph	**Hanna's Graph**
Cats		
Dogs		
Fish		
Lizards		
Other		

b) Do the graphs show the same information? _____

Do the graphs look the same? _____

c) How did Jake choose to order the labels on the horizontal axis?

_____

How did Hanna choose to order the labels on the horizontal axis?

_____

d) Which pet was the most common? _____

On which graph is it easier to see that? _____

3. Sara is researching different dog breeds.

a) Fill in the table using Bar Graph I.

Dog Breed	Weight (lb)
Beagle (B)	
Collie (C)	
Dalmatian (D)	
Husky (H)	
Pug (P)	

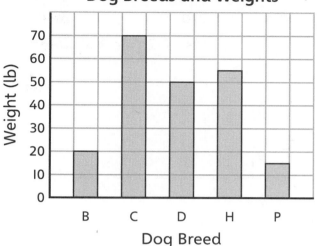

Bar Graph I
Dog Breeds and Weights

b) What number does the scale

skip count by? _____

c) Are there bars that end between the numbers? _____

d) How many blocks long is the tallest bar? _____

e) Use the table to finish Bar Graph 2 with a scale that skip counts by 5 to show the same information.

f) Are there bars that end between

the numbers? _____

g) Which graph takes more space? _____

h) Use the graphs to say which dog breed weighs 20 lb more than a dalmatian.

_____

Which graph makes this easier

to answer? _____

i) Use the graphs to find out which breed weighs 55 lb less than a collie.

_____

Which graph makes this easier

to answer? _____

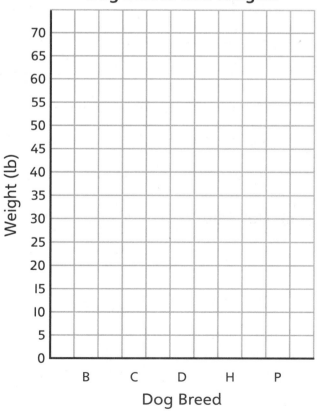

Bar Graph 2
Dog Breeds and Weights

Some bar graphs are not drawn on a grid.

This bar graph shows that Vicky has 10 snakes and 5 iguanas.

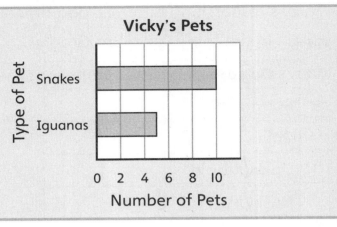

Vicky's Pets

4. Students voted for their favorite breakfast.

   a) Fill in the table.

Type of Food	Number of Students
Cereal	
Eggs	
Pancakes	
Toast	
Waffles	

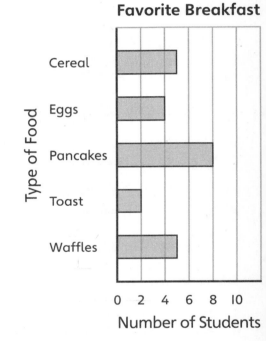

Favorite Breakfast

   b) How many more students voted

      for pancakes than cereal? _____

   c) How many fewer students voted for eggs

      than waffles? _____

5. Grade 3 students collected cans of food for a food bank for a week. They showed the results in a bar graph.

   a) How many more cans were collected on Friday than on Monday?

   b) How many fewer cans were collected on Tuesday and Wednesday together than on Friday?

   c) How many cans were collected in total?

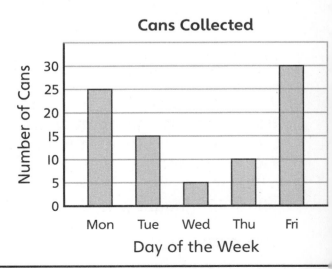

Cans Collected